THE ESSENTIAL GUIDE TO

HORSE CARE

THE ESSENTIAL GUIDE TO

HORSE CARE

Amanda Edwards

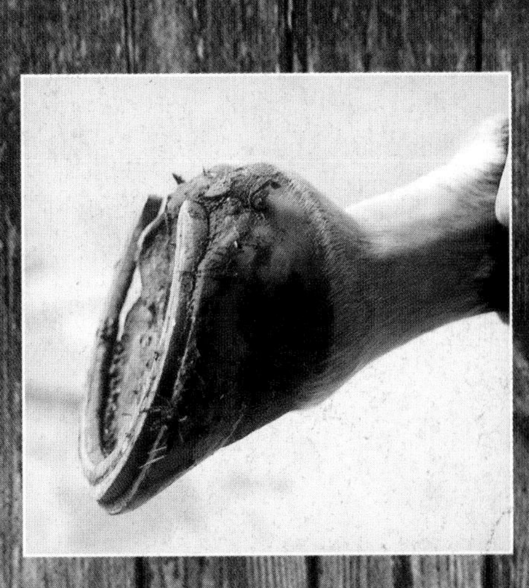

Abbeydale Press

Published in 1998 by
Abbeydale Press
An imprint of Bookmart Limited
Desford Road
Enderby
Leicester
LE9 5AD

ISBN 1 86147020 7

Printed in Spain

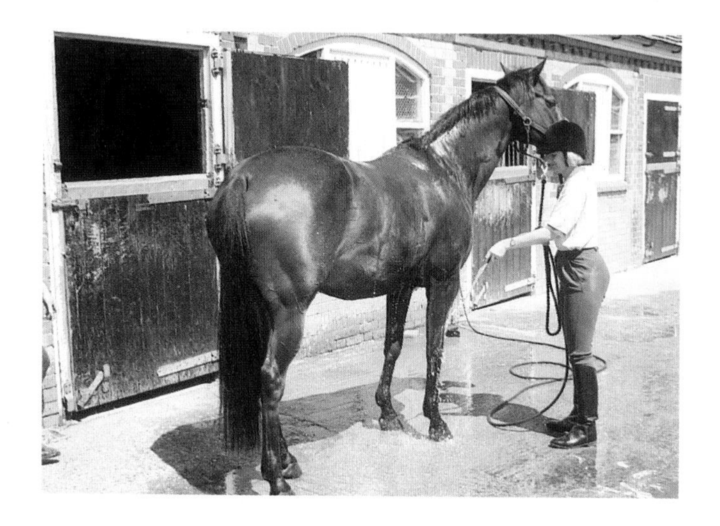

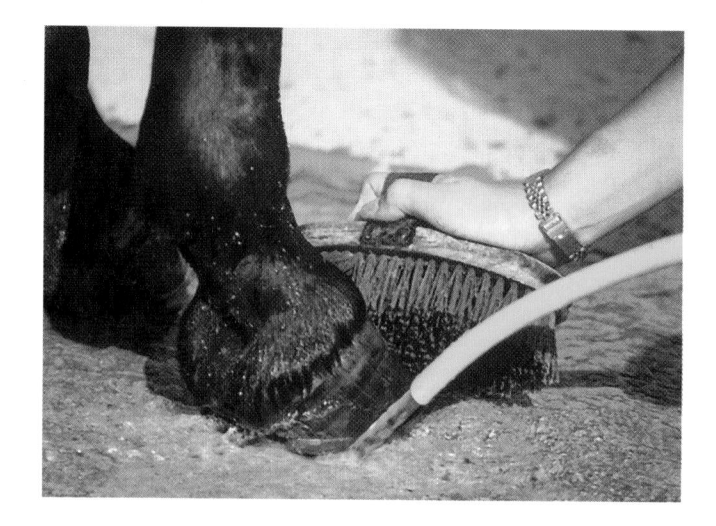

CONTENTS

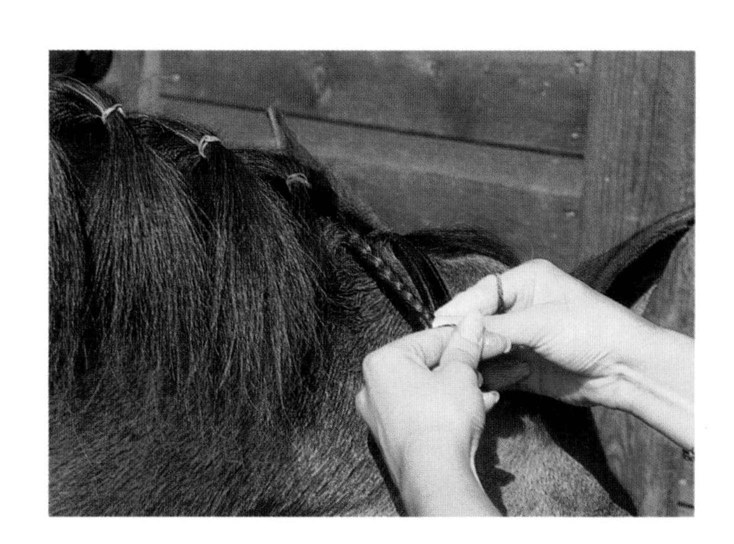

▲ Given sufficient care and attention, your horse will stay in excellent condition throughout the winter, whether it is stabled or at grass.

INTRODUCTION

Throughout the centuries, the horse has proved itself indispensable to mankind. As late as the 1940s, its importance as a working animal on farms, in mining, in time of war, and as a vital means of transportation could not be over-emphasized. A good horse has therefore always been highly esteemed and even today has a valuable contribution to make on ranches and sheep stations in the American and Australian continents.

Nowadays, however, working horses are rarely seen and heavy work-horses are rather more common in the show-ring than pulling a plough.

Horses are now mainly kept for pleasure, being of particular benefit to disabled riders as a way of increasing spatial awareness and co-ordination. The army still uses horses, though more for ceremonial purposes these days.

Riding is now one of the top five sports, with livery yards and riding schools proliferating. Selective breeding is now producing an athletic horse, capable of great stamina and agility in the dressage arena, in show-jumping and in three-day eventing.

Many people now own or have the loan of a horse, and a comprehensive understanding of its needs is vital to its well-being. Caring for a horse is a large and complex subject; but much can be learned by observation and learning to profit from your own experience.

This is a basic outline of the correct procedure, along with useful tips to ensure that your association with your horse is a happy and contented one.

▼ Remember, that keeping a horse consumes a great deal of time and energy. However, given the correct feeding, exercise and grooming, your horse will achieve as fine a level of condition as this one.

POINTS OF THE HORSE

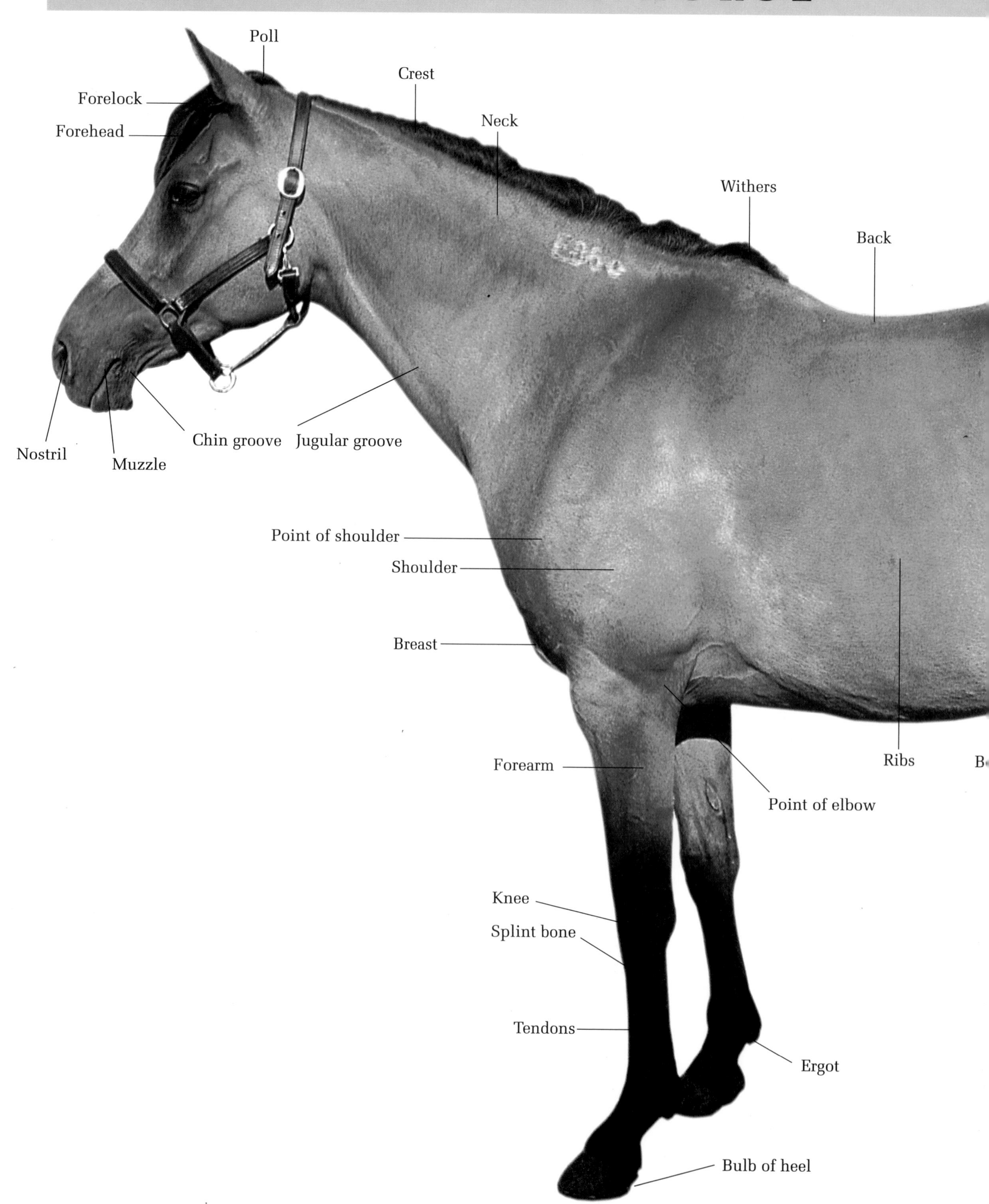

It is a good idea to memorize the points of the horse; you will then know what is being discussed when conformation is mentioned – particularly when buying a horse or talking to a vet.

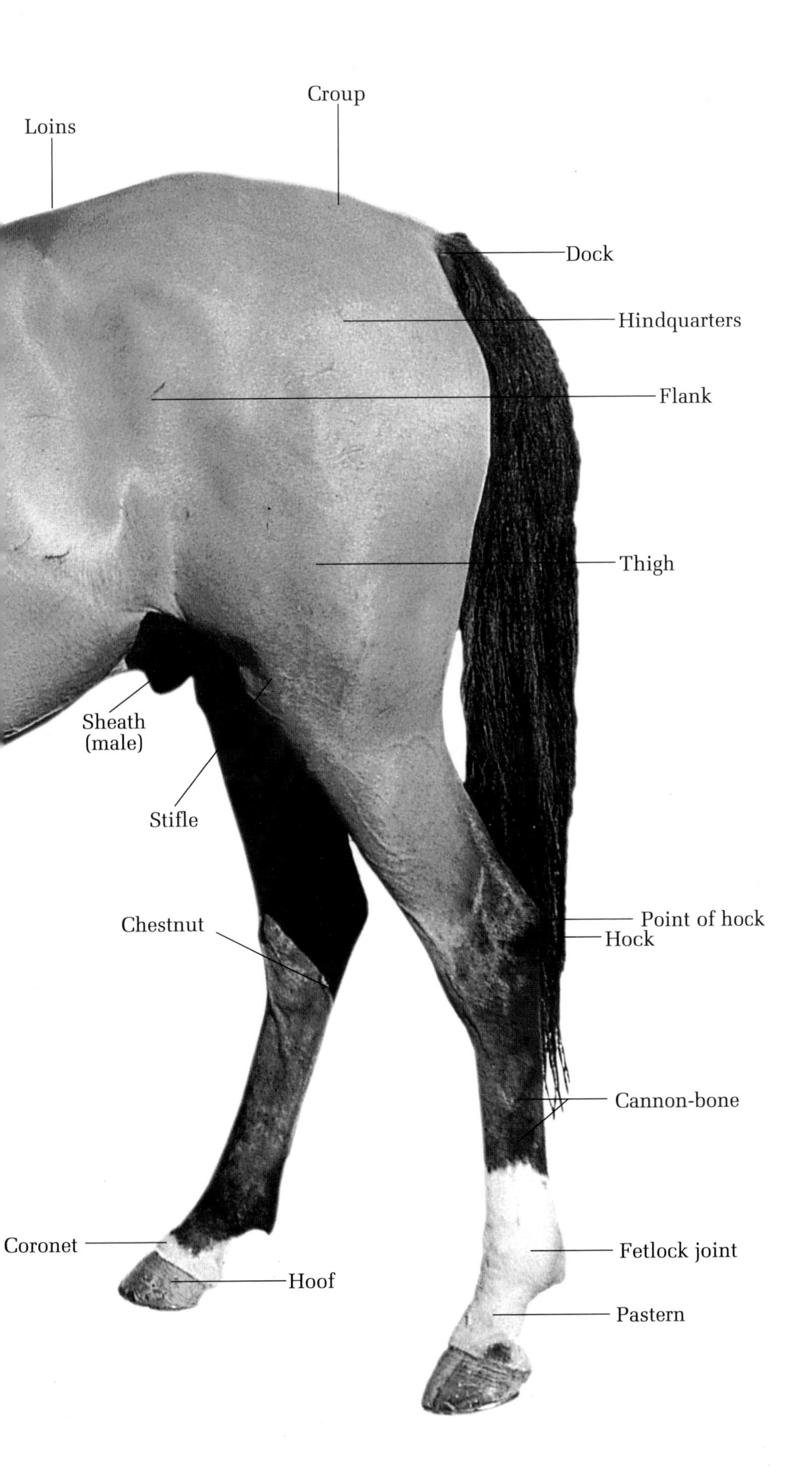

CONFORMATION

When considering buying a horse of your own, it is important that you recognize what is meant by a good one by studying the way the animal is put together: this is known as the horse's 'conformation'. Horses come in many shapes and sizes, but whatever the type, whether Shetland pony or Thoroughbred, the basic rules of conformation still apply.

First study the horse from a distance. The overall effect should be one of symmetry and balance. The head should not be too large nor the back too long. The shoulder should be gently sloping and the neck long and graceful with a well developed crest. The legs should be straight and clean with good-sized joints. Make sure that the animal stands foursquare and look at it from the back, checking that the hind-legs are level with the fore-legs and that its quarters are even. The tail should be set high and the buttocks well developed as this is vital for good propulsion. Look for a deep chest with plenty of space for heart and lungs.

Now take a closer look. Check that legs are free from lumps and bumps caused by old injuries. Hooves should be symmetrical, free from cracks or ridges and have plenty of heel. Avoid large horses with small feet as the horse's weight concentrated on a smaller area will mean that concussion will be more and shock absorption less, leading to possible lameness. The coat should be bright and glossy and gleaming with health. The head is a good indication of character. Look for an alert expression, with pricked ears and a head well set on the neck. The eyes should be bright, clear and kind. A rolling eye is a possible indication of instability or that a horse is sick. A piggy eye – one with too much white showing – is often thought to indicate a mean nature; but there are exceptions to every rule and the most unlikely horse can turn out to be surprisingly talented, proving that first impressions are not invariably correct.

◀ Good conformation is important if your horse is to stay sound and healthy. When choosing a horse, follow the basic rules closely as this will help you spot defects such as weak hocks, poor feet, or a 'ewe-neck'. Once you have found the horse which is perfect for your needs you can look forward to a happy and rewarding partnership.

▼ Through selective breeding, horses have been developed to fulfil specific functions. This Thoroughbred racehorse has been bred for great speed and stamina.

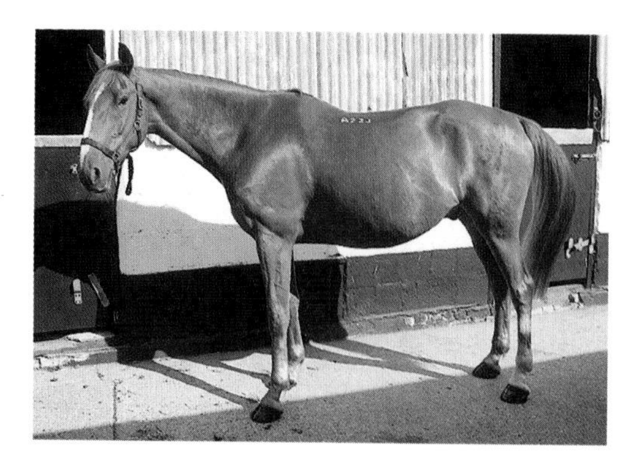

A long back (long in the back) is a sign of weakness. The horse may have difficulty tracking-up, making engagement difficult; but this is not necessarily always the case.

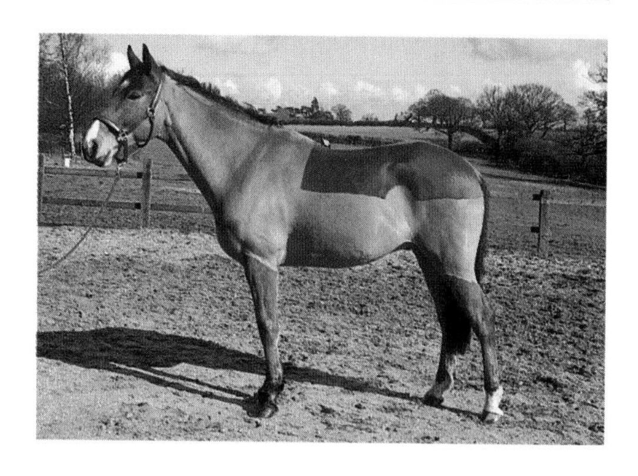

A horse with a short back can encounter problems such as overreaching, and it can be difficult to fit a saddle correctly. However, horses such as these often have natural good balance, making them ideal for the twists and turns of the show-jumping course.

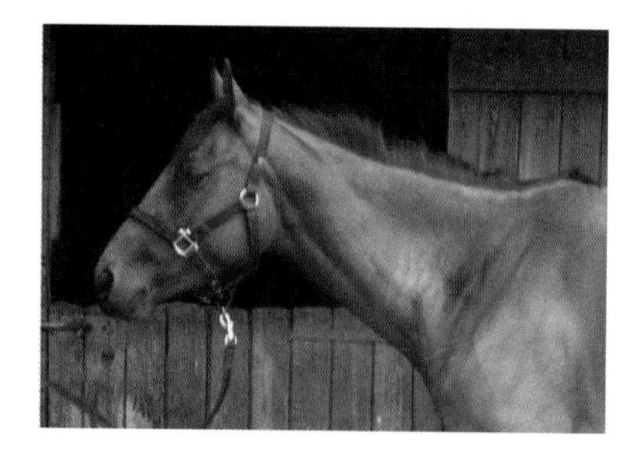

A 'ewe-neck' is considered to be a bad defect of conformation to the extent that the horse may have difficulty working in a rounded outline and accepting the bridle.

Defects to Watch Out For

The Legs If the horse is to stay sound and maintain a good action, it is important that it has well shaped legs. If the fore-legs are 'over at the knee' or 'back at the knee', for example, its weight will be unevenly distributed. This may cause extra strain on localized areas such as the heel, just as toes turning in or out can cause strain on the pastern, fetlock and foot.

The same applies to the hind-legs: hocks tucked under or which are too far behind the body interfere with propulsion. Cow hocks and bowed hocks are also a sign of weakness and horses with such defects should be avoided.

The Back When ridden, a horse's back is asked to take a good deal of strain; therefore, it is vital that it is as strong as possible and good muscle development obviously has a lot to do with this. However, the horse's basic structure and general conformation is also important. Avoid a horse with a long or 'sway' back, which is a sign of weakness. Also avoid a *very* short back as the rider's weight could end up on the horse's loins, which is the most vulnerable part of the back.

The Head and Neck. A horse with a large head can be a problem to school as it may have difficulty keeping in balance. Avoid one which has a 'ewe-neck'. This means that the horse's lower neck is bulkier and more developed that the crest, making it look as though it is on upside-down. This is very difficult or even impossible to correct. A 'bull-neck' – one which is short and thick – is also problematical, and it will be difficult to obtain sufficient flexion when riding such a horse.

Breeds and Types

Horses and ponies belong to these two specific groups. A **breed** consists of horses or ponies which are genetically similar and have been selectively bred to produce consistent characteristics while reinforcing their best features, and recognized as such in official stud books. They fall into four distinct classes: 'hotbloods' – highly-strung animals such as Thoroughbreds and Arabs which are suited to racing and fast work; 'warmbloods' – slightly heavier animals bred for their extravagant paces and which are excellent performers in dressage and jumping. This is the result of interbreeding with heavier 'coldbloods' such as Shires and Cleveland Bays, which give them rather more placid temperaments than hotbloods. Lastly, there is the native breed of under 14.2hh in height – the pony. A **type**, however, is the result of interbreeding to produce horses for specific purposes and can include cobs, hunters and colour-types such as Palominos.

▶ A cob type is ideal for anyone requiring strength and dependability. They are very hardy and are usually 'good doers'.

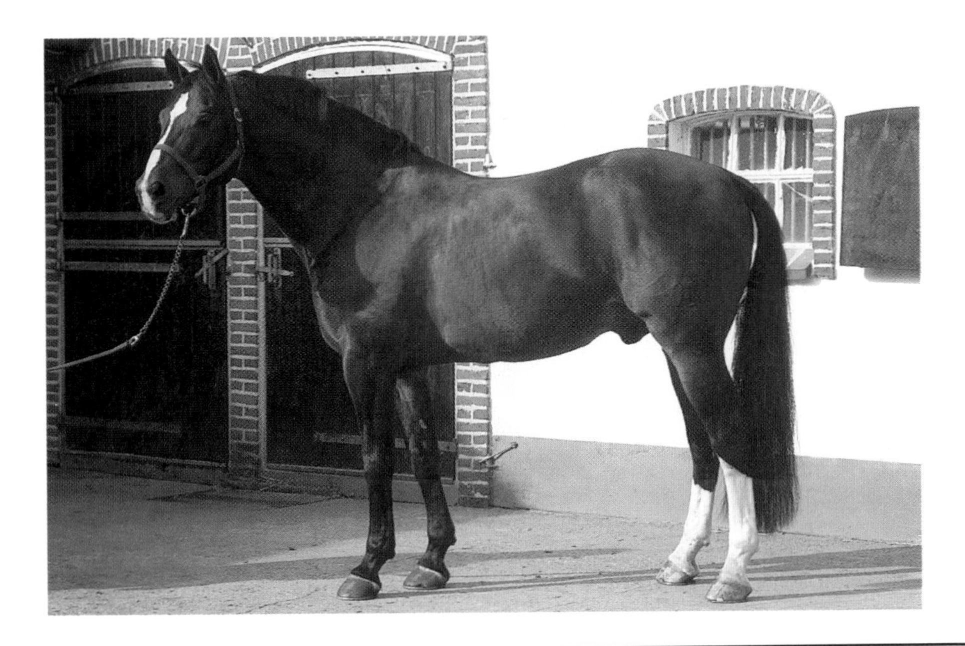

◀ Warmbloods are much more sedate than Thoroughbreds, their equitable nature and beautiful natural paces making them ideal for dressage.

◀ Officially, a pony is anything under 14.2hh. It usually derives from native breeds such as the Welsh mountain, Dartmoor and Shetland. Showing ponies both in-hand and ridden is popular with children and adults alike.

CONFORMATION

◀ The graceful Thoroughbred is bred for its speed and stamina. It is said to have orginated from three Arab stallions in the early 18th century, the Byerly Turk, the Darley Arabian and the Godolphin Arabian which were bred with British racing mares to produce the breed.

Coat Colours

Horses and ponies come in a variety of colours, developed through selective breeding.

The Bay has a coat of reddish-brown with black on the lower legs, muzzle and tips of the ears. The mane and tail are also black.

The Brown is dark brown all over.

The Chestnut has a reddish-brown coat with a mane and tail of a similar colour.

The Liver Chestnut is a darker version of the chestnut.

The Dun is rarer and consists of a sandy-coloured coat with black lower legs and muzzle and a black mane and tail.

The Black has a completely black coat, mane and tail.

The Palomino has a beautiful golden coat with a white mane and tail.

The Cream has a cream coat, mane and tail.

The Grey varies from white, dappled

▲ The coloured horse is becoming very popular. Horses with black-and-white markings are classified as piebalds while those with other colours with white are known as skewbalds.

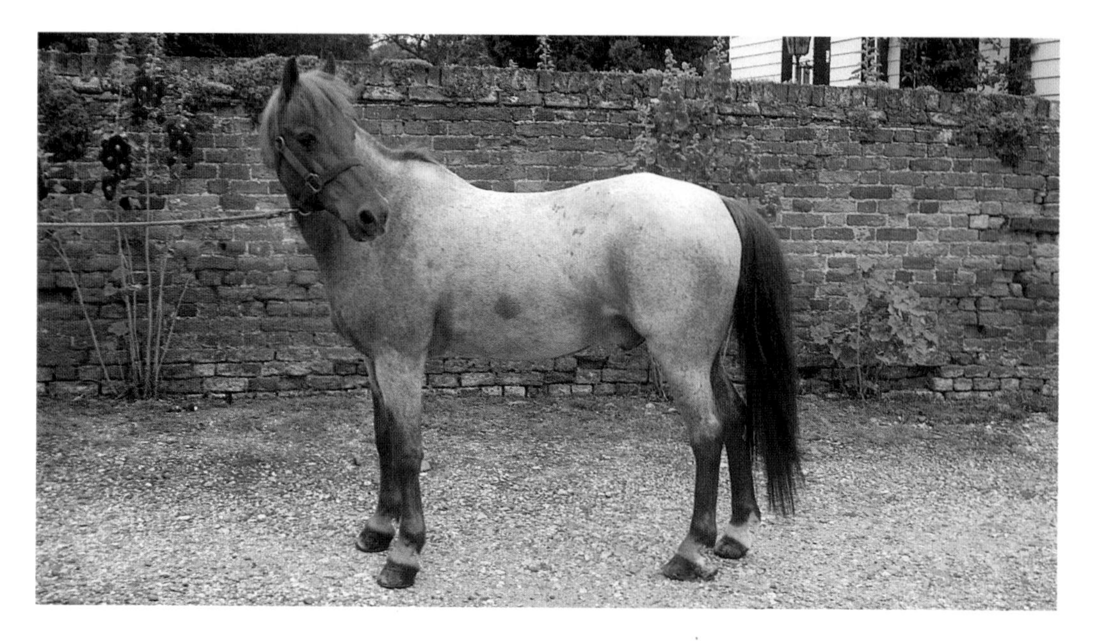

▶ This pretty pony is a strawberry roan, having chestnut with flecks of white in its coat.

and iron to flea-bitten. Most grey horses get whiter as they get older, though are still referred to as grey.

The Roan has white hairs intermingled with the main colour of the coat and there are three types: strawberry roan, which is chestnut; red roan which is bay; and blue roan which is black – all mixed with white.

The Spotted has a grey coat with either brown or black spots, usually called appaloosa. There is also a breed of this name which bears these markings.

Skewbald is a coat of any colour (except black) patched with white.

Piebald is a coat consisting of black-and-white patches.

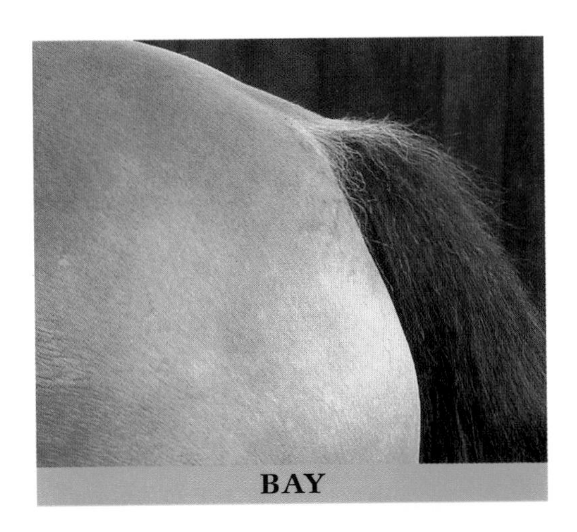
BAY

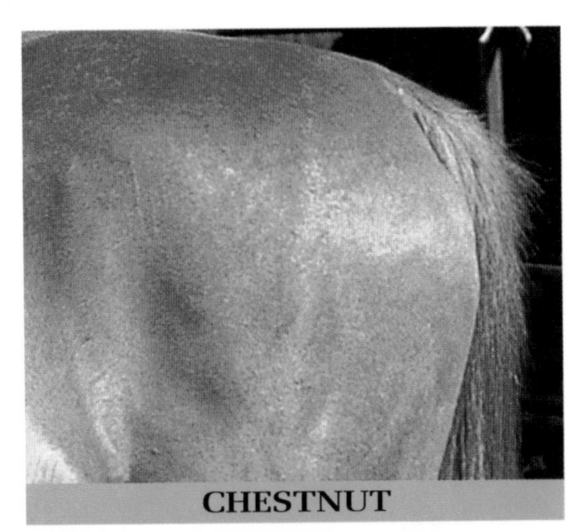
CHESTNUT

◄ The original wild horses would have had dull brown coats to help them blend into their environment. Today's horses have brighter coloured coats, achieved through selective breeding.

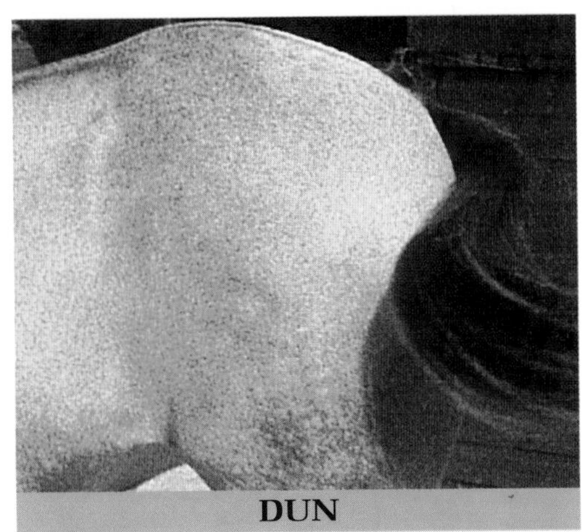
DUN

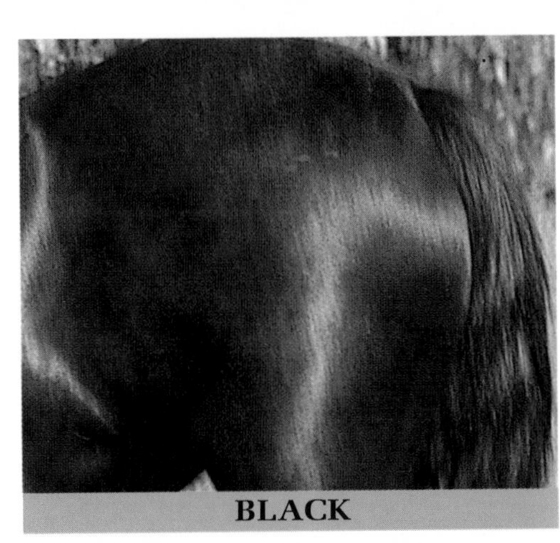
BLACK

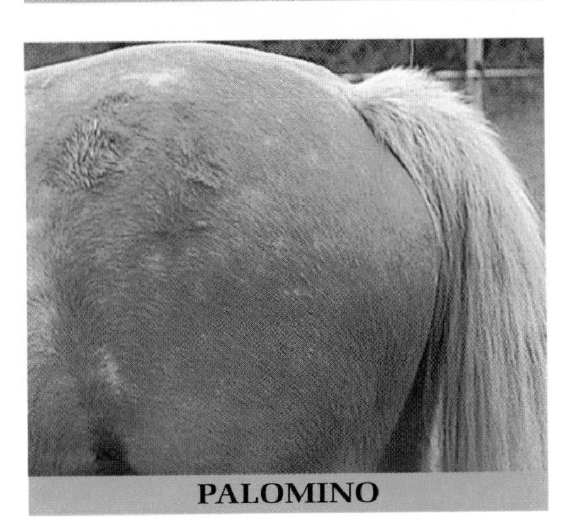
PALOMINO

GREY

MARKINGS

A horse's markings are useful for recognition, especially from a distance. If your horse has been freeze-marked, or has a passport, his markings will have been carefully noted to distinguish him from any other horse.

Face markings

STAR & SNIP, JOINED

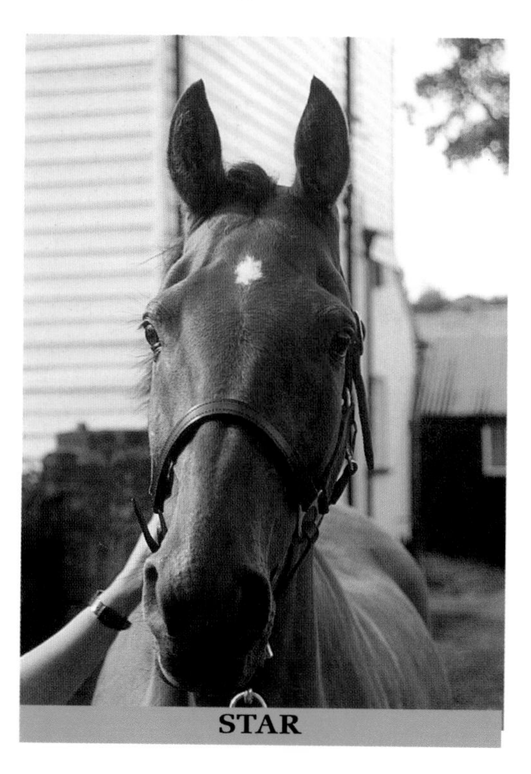

STAR

BLAZE

◀ Whatever your horse's markings, they are an essential part of his character. This horse has face markings somewhere halfway between a star and blaze.

Leg markings

Socks extend up to the fetlock joint.
Stockings extend up the cannon-bone up to the knee.
Ermine refers to the black spots on the white fur of the coronet.

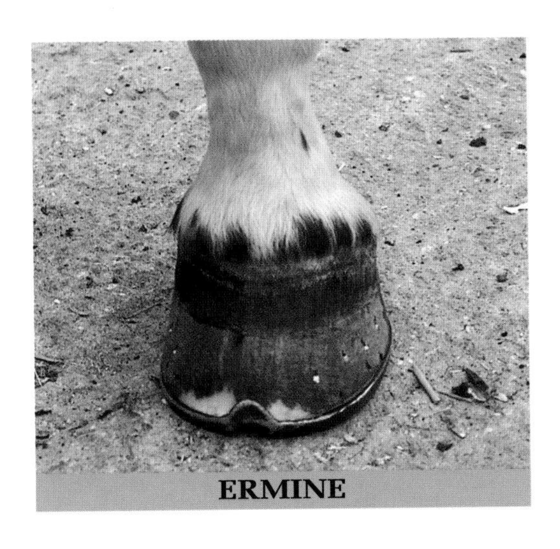

ERMINE

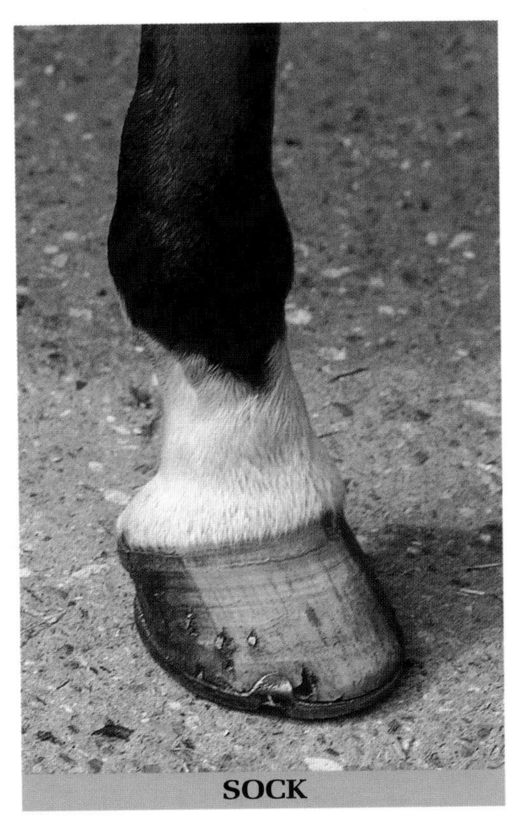

SOCK

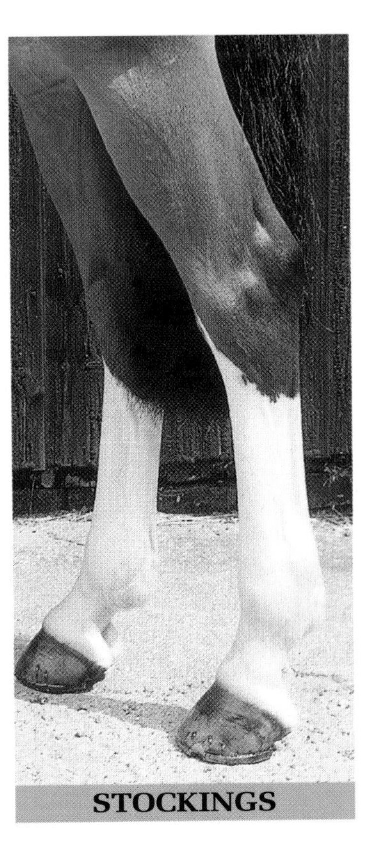

STOCKINGS

CHOOSING THE RIGHT HORSE

Before deciding to buy a horse of your own you should be proficient in the saddle and have a sound practical knowledge of horse care. The best way to learn these skills is at a riding school and it is possible to attend courses on stable management. Ignorance, however unintentional, is not only dangerous but can lead to cruelty, abuse and neglect.

You will also need to be aware of the cost involved: buying a horse is just the beginning. Keeping a horse is an expensive business and you must make allowances for veterinary bills, shoeing, tack, rugs and other equipment. Horses are very time-consuming: carefully decide beforehand how much time you can spare each day. There are different types of livery available which vary in cost from full livery, where your horse is completely cared for by another qualified person, to do-it-yourself where responsibility for all the animal's needs is completely your own.

Once you have established that you can afford the time and financial commitment, you can look for a horse which is suitable for your level of competence and requirements. Before you begin, you must think very carefully. It is inappropriate to buy a flashy and lively Thoroughbred if you only have a basic level of riding skill: on the other hand, a person who can already ride well and has the confidence to compete will be disappointed with a horse of limited ability and will swiftly outgrow it.

The type of horse you eventually choose should be the right size for you. You should ensure that you can ride it safely and confidently and that the accommodation you have arranged for it is suitable. For example, if you know that it will spend a large amount of time turned out in a field, go for a much hardier type.

Where to look Once all these factors have been considered, you can begin your search for a horse. Beware of the

▶ Before deciding to buy a horse, it is important that you acquire some knowledge of horse care as well as adequate riding skills. Make sure you choose a horse that is the right size for you and suited to your level of ability.

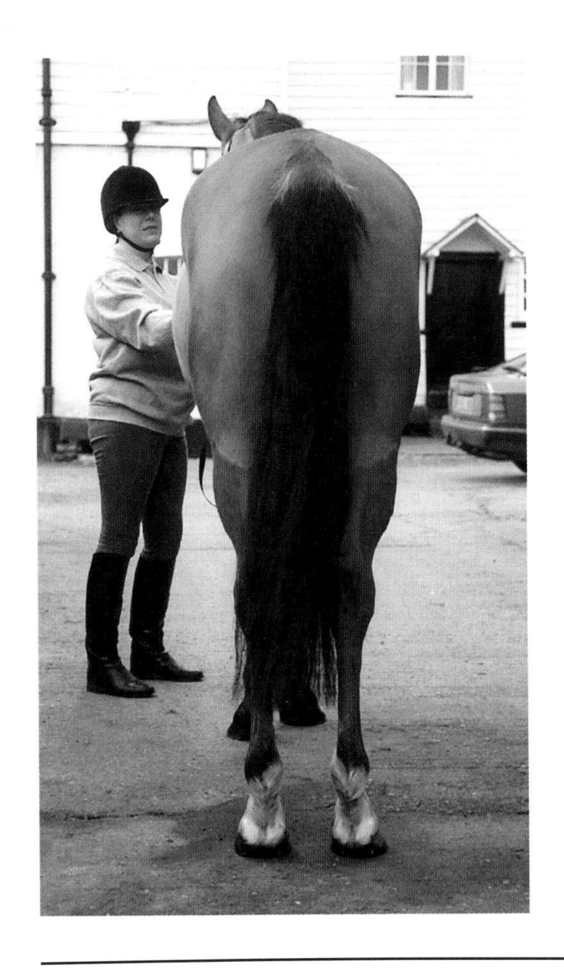

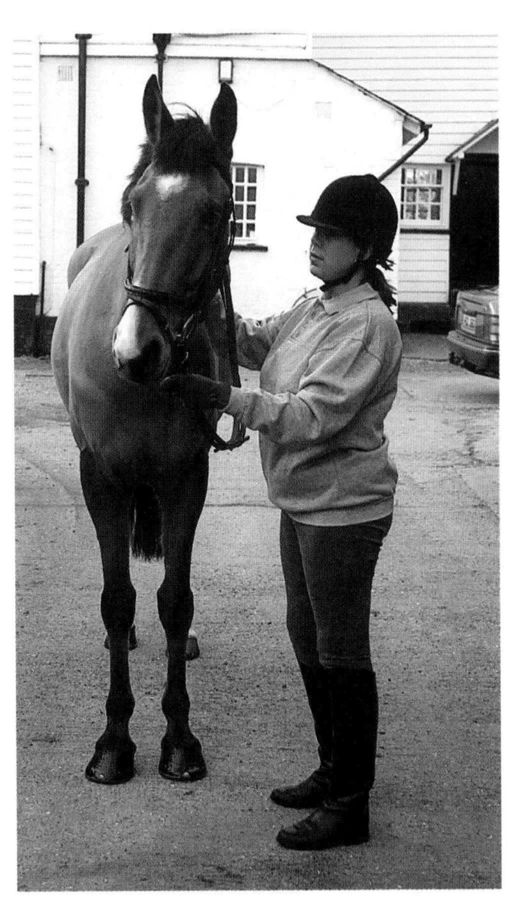

◀ Looking at a horse standing square can reveal many potential problems. If it appears lopsided, it may have some muscle wastage due to an old injury. Common conformation defects such as cow hocks and pigeon toes may also become apparent.

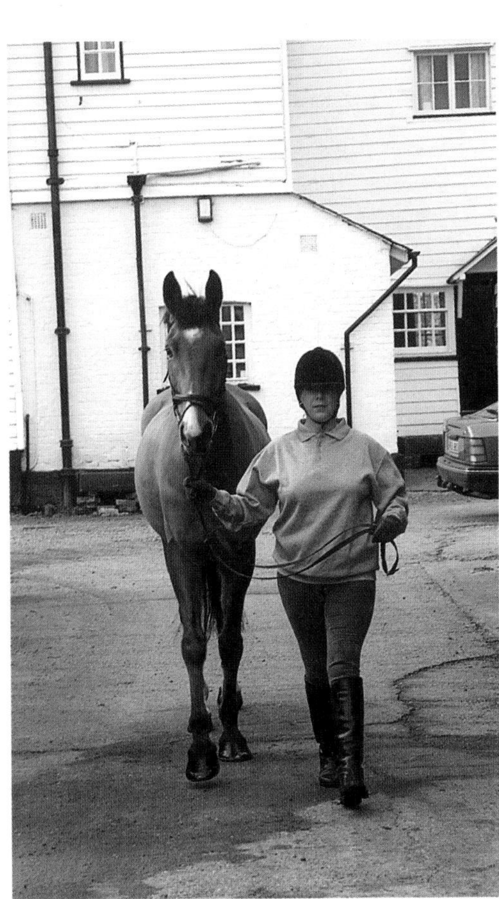

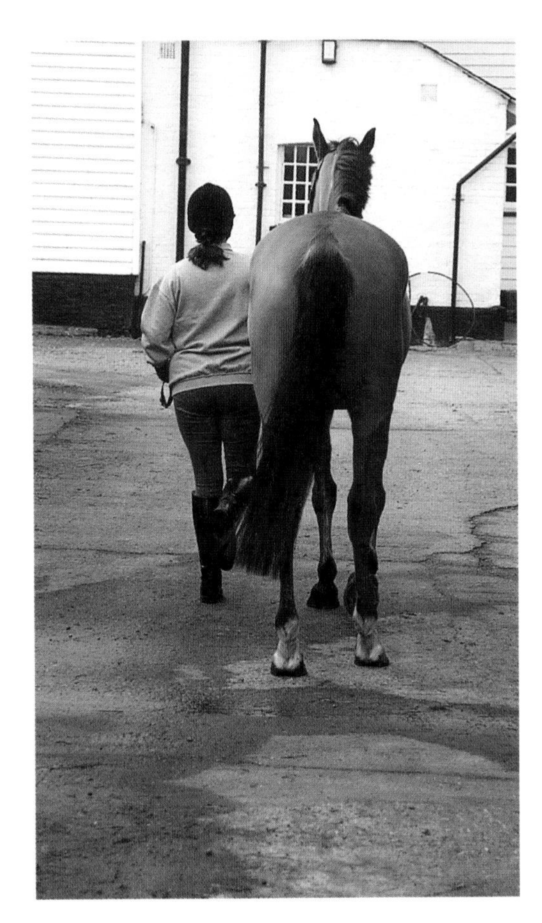

◀ Trotting a horse up will reveal any obvious signs of lameness as well as faults of conformation, such as dishing (where the front legs turn outwards at trot). You will also be able to confirm that the horse has straight action, an important attribute in any horse.

To pick up on more obscure signs of lameness and other faults of action, it is a good idea to view the horse when it is being lunged, both on hard and soft going.

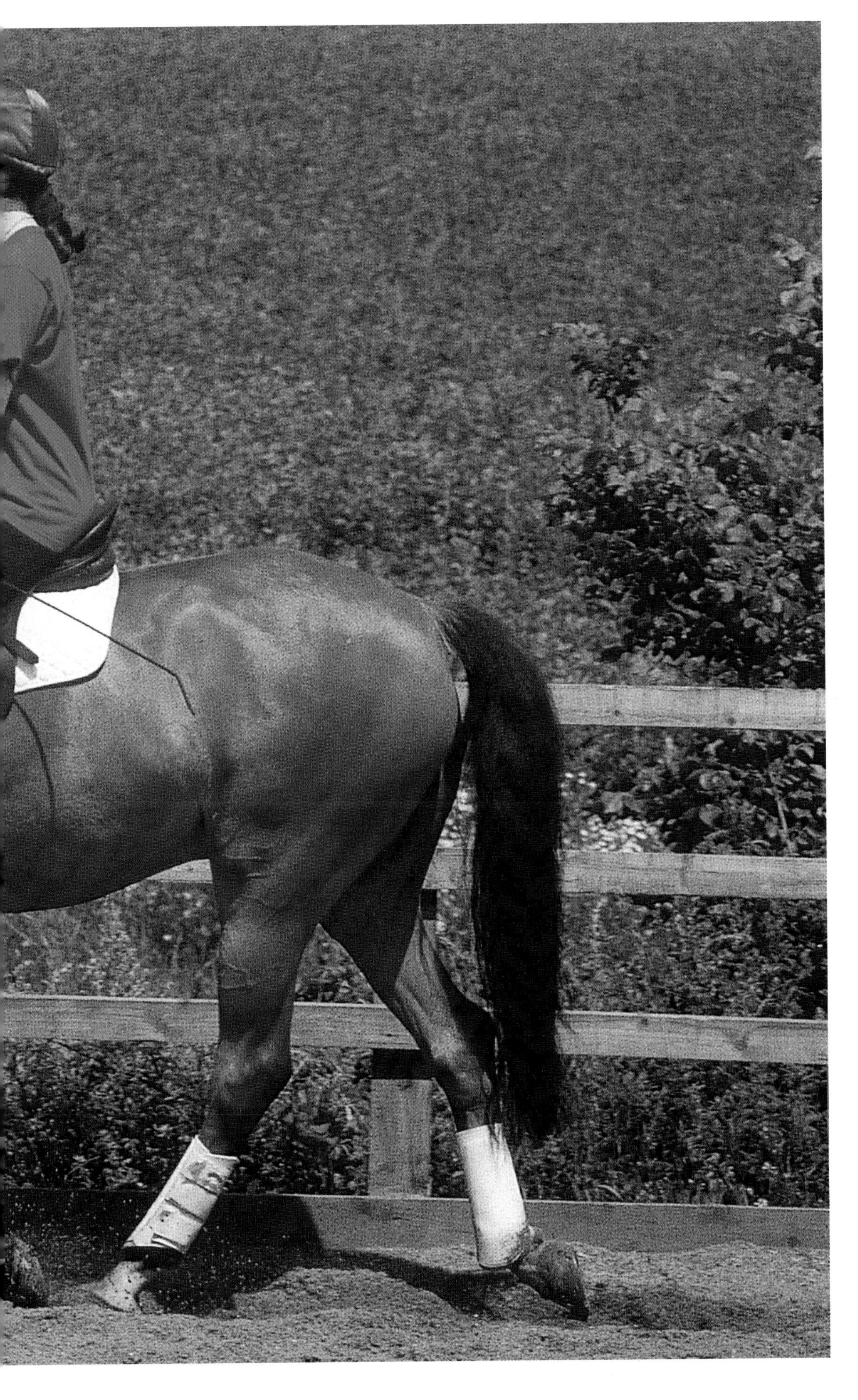

◀ Once you have established that the horse you wish to buy is sound and suitable, try it out. First, however, ask its owner to ride it, then an experienced friend; this will enable you to see what its action and temperament is like from a safe distance.

If there is a school on the premises, use it, putting the horse through its paces and, if you are so inclined, over a couple of small jumps. This will give you an idea of the horse's willingness to go forward.

Next, you will need to see how it behaves on public roads: a traffic-shy horse is a liability and extremely dangerous.

Do not attempt to ride a strange horse in traffic yourself until you are sure it is safe.

▶ A kind eye is a good indicator of a horse's nature. A mean look can suggest bad temper.

pitfalls: you are likely to be spending a great deal of money on what is after all a living creature, so always take a knowledgeable person with you. It is a good idea to buy a horse from a person or establishment with a good reputation; this could, for example, be the riding school where you learned to ride. Take a look at the notice boards of other riding establishments and saddlery shops or ask an experienced person if they are aware of any suitable horses for sale. There are many horse magazines with classified sections available, but stick to private sales if possible – you are more likely to get an accurate picture of the horse's past form. Most reputable dealers will have a good selection of horses but are unlikely to know as much about them, and they are often very expensive. Avoid horse sales unless you are very experienced.

What to ask and look out for Once you have found a horse that interests you, ask the owner as many pertinent questions as possible in order to obtain as full a picture as you can of the horse's history, and from every point of view. Make a list of the questions you need to ask beforehand. Find out if it suffers from any ailments or has any stable vices. Ask what it is usually fed and what bedding is habitually used – this can often indicate that it is suffering from a stable allergy.

First look at the horse in its stable; check that it is calm and happy in its surroundings. Give it a pat and make its acquaintance over the stable door, noting if it attempts to bite or has its ears laid back. Check that it is standing on all four legs; a rested limb can be a sign of lameness. Then ask the owner to get it out of its stable so that you can look it over carefully, remembering the rules of conformation. Ask the owner to trot the horse up to check that it is sound and moving straight. Once this is established it can then be tacked up.

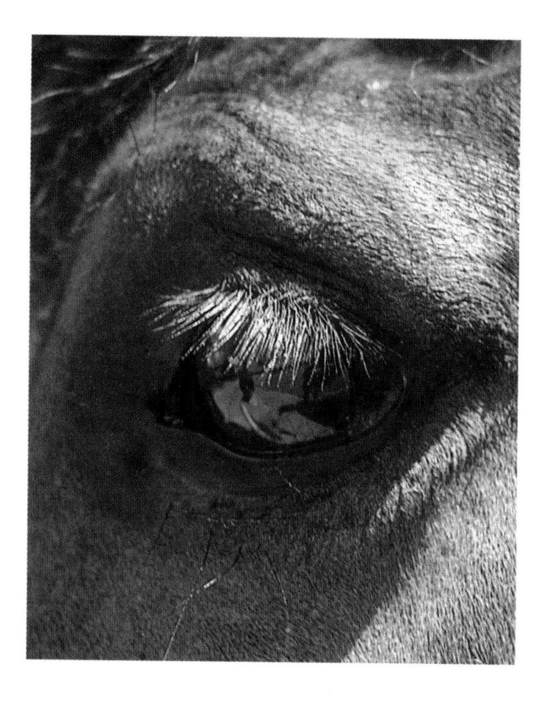

Trying him out Check the tack; what type of bit is the horse wearing? A severe bit is an indication that he is a bit of a handful. What kind of pad has been placed under the saddle? Too much padding and he could have back problems. Now ask to see him ridden: always ask the vendor to warm the horse up first – it is not a good idea to get onto an unknown animal straightaway. Next ask your experienced friend to try him and once you feel reassured, try him yourself, putting him through his paces and trying a few small jumps. If you are happy so far, insist that you see him ridden in traffic as a traffic-shy horse will be useless if you wish to enjoy hacking out.

Some vendors will let you take the horse on a trial basis; always ask if you can do this before committing yourself to a sale. This is an excellent idea because, if the vendor agrees to the proposal it will prove that he has confidence in the horse and indicates his genuineness.

Vetting If all appears well so far, the next stage will be to get the horse vetted, preferably by your own veterinary surgeon. It is best if you are present as the vet may wish to discuss certain relevant points with you. A full vetting is expensive but is money well spent; it is necessary for insurance as insurers will insist on a certificate of soundness before issuing a policy. The vet will check the horse's sight and soundness in leg, heart and wind; he will check that the horse is moving well and that he has good flexion in all his limbs. He will also be able to check the age of the animal by looking at his teeth, although it is only possible to gauge this with any certainty up to the age of 8. After this, there are more approximate indications. The horse will then be galloped and checked once again as this is likely to reveal signs of lameness as well as respiratory and/or heart problems. Once this has been done and the horse has been passed as fit, only then will a certificate of soundness be issued. Further tests may be advised if there is any evidence of unsoundness, and x-rays will reveal diseases such as navicular syndrome and signs of arthritis. A blood test will produce evidence that the horse has been drugged and may be desirable if marked fluctuations of temperament during the process of the sale are noticed. These tests are an added expense but are no doubt worth it for the extra peace of mind they give.

Once you have made your choice the hard work begins; but having established a close relationship you will find your partnership with your horse both rewarding and fun.

▼ Buying a pony for a child is full of pitfalls if you have little experience of horses yourself. Always seek expert advice and never be tempted to buy unless you are fully committed to the animal's welfare. Do not forget that in a very short time a child will quickly outgrow what was previously perfectly suitable for him. Remember: keeping a horse or pony is an expensive business, so look before you leap.

Maintaining your horse in good health can only be achieved by correct feeding, sufficient exercise and good stable management. Try to develop a keen eye: good powers of observation are invaluable in assessing your horse's overall condition.

Check him over once a day – a good time to do this is when you are grooming him. Check that his eyes are bright and shining and that his expression is alert. Make sure that he is breathing steadily and in a relaxed manner. As you groom, run your hands over body and legs, feeling for any lumps or signs of inflammation which could indicate that he has been kicked when out in the field, or has pulled a tendon. Pick the feet out twice a day or whenever necessary, checking for puncture wounds, bruising or stones that have become embedded and make

WARNING SIGNS OF ILLNESS

Learn to recognize the signs that your horse is unwell. This will come with experience as you get to know him intimately as an individual. Any of the symptoms listed below could be indications of colic, asthma or pain resulting from lameness. In addition, check him over carefully for signs of any external damage, then call the vet.

- sweating
- rolling of the eyes
- heavy breathing
- tucking in at the flanks
- looking towards or pecking at the stomach
- a dejected look
- loose faeces
- resting one leg more than the other

Correct feeding and exercise will help keep your horse healthy. However, when things do go wrong, learn to recognize the signs and act quickly. Neglecting to call the vet when necessary is worse than calling him out too early.

sure that the frogs of the hooves are healthy with no signs of thrush or foot rot. Trot him up to check for soundness.

Tetanus and equine influenza are both very serious diseases and it is vital that your horse is protected against them by vaccination. Regular worming (about every 6 weeks) is also important as infestation can seriously undermine a horse's constitution and even cause death. Young horses, mares and foals will require a special worming programme.

Regular shoeing is also vital if your horse is to stay sound, as well as periodical mouth checks to ensure that there are no injuries caused by rubbing bits. Check also that teeth do not need rasping – this could impair chewing ability and mastication of food.

THE VITAL SIGNS

Learn to recognize when your horse is breathing normally. A horse's respiration at rest will on average be 8–16 breaths per minute. A breath is one in–out movement and can be gauged by looking at or feeling the rib cage. Rapid breathing at rest is a sure indication that a horse is distressed and is very likely to be in pain.

Taking the temperature. First shake down the thermometer and apply petroleum jelly to it. Standing to the side, insert the thermometer and press it gently to the side wall of the rectum. Hold it in place for the prescribed amount of time (check instructions). The horse's normal temperature is 37.5–38°C (99.5–100.4°F). A rise of a degree should be taken seriously.

Checking the pulse. This can be taken at various sites – behind the pastern and to either side of the fetlock (the digital pulse) or you can use a stethoscope behind the elbow. The easiest place to feel the pulse is where the artery crosses the inside edge of the jaw-bone. Use only your fingers, and lightly, as your thumb has a strong pulse of its own. Normal pulse at rest is 36–40 beats per minute. Increased pulse and respiration when at rest may be caused by excitement, stress, pain or illness.

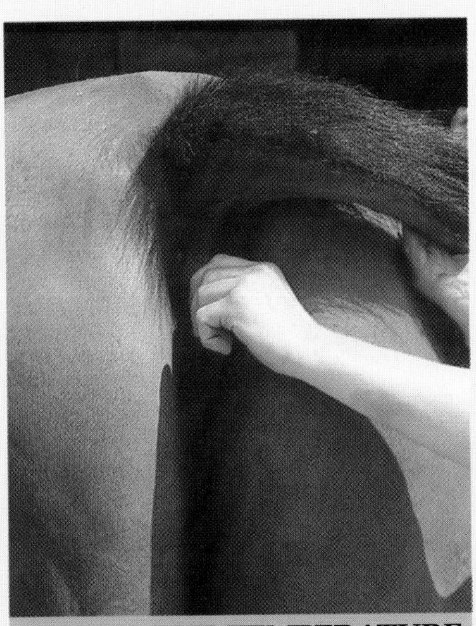

TAKING THE TEMPERATURE

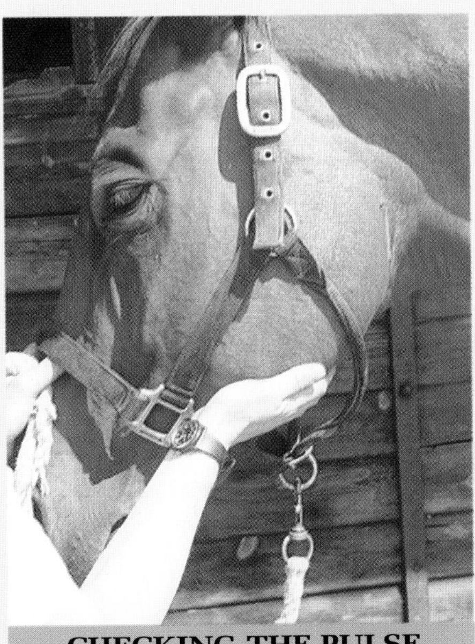

CHECKING THE PULSE

Respiratory Disorders

Chronic obstructive pulmonary disease (COPD) This is caused by an allergy to the fungal spores present in hay and straw which sets off the condition. The horse will have trouble breathing and will have a cough and usually a nasal discharge. He will attempt to free his lungs, with obvious heaving movements of the chest. COPD can be prevented by keeping the horse on alternative bedding (such as wood-shavings), feeding haylage or soaked hay, and turning the horse out of the stable as much as possible. In severe cases, a drug can be administered to open up the airways. **Call the vet.**

Equine influenza This is a particularly unpleasant viral infection which can be fatal to very young, old, or weak horses and survivors can be left with chronic heart and lung problems as a result. The horse develops a high temperature, runny eyes and nose and a cough. Once infected, there is little effective treatment other than giving drugs to keep the airways open. A simple yearly vaccination will help prevent the disease occurring in the first place. **Isolate and call the vet.**

Roaring and whistling This is a throat condition in which paralysis of the muscles of the larynx restricts the airflow through the trachea. The horse shows no sign of malaise until strenuously exercised when a loud roaring sound will be heard as the horse breathes in. This will usually affect its performance. It is a condition horses are often born with, and surgery may be necessary in severe cases when the vocal cord is permanently pulled back out of the way. **Ask your vet's advice.**

Strangles This is a highly contagious bacterial infection of the jowl region and has an incubation period of 6 weeks. Large abscesses break out under the horse's jaw, accompanied by a high temperature. Eventually the abscesses burst, releasing a foul-smelling pus. Sometimes they burst internally, resulting in pus being released through the nose. Treatment is by antibiotics and the abscesses can be treated as ordinary wounds once they have burst. The condition can prove fatal if the infection is allowed to spread to the lymphatic system when it may cause internal abcesses in the thorax and abdomen. The disease is then known as 'bastard strangles'. **Isolate and call the vet.**

Circulatory Disorders

Azoturia Also described as 'set fast' or 'tying-up', this is caused by too much food and too little exercise and is the result of keeping an often very fit horse on a full working diet when it is confined to stable, or having a rest day. The horse will appear stiff and obviously uncomfortable when next exercised, the large muscles of the back and hindquarters becoming very hard and swollen. Dark, port wine-coloured urine may also be passed. The cause of this is the ineffective breakdown of sugars in the muscles which causes a build-up of lactic acid. This is a serious condition as lactic acid cannot easily be removed by the circulation, causing damage to the muscles and possibly to the kidneys. Immobilize the horse, putting rugs on him to warm him up

Sore and streaming eyes can be an indication of illness or, in summer, of fly damage.

and which will help increase the circulation. **Call the vet.**

Lymphangitis Physical evidence is a very swollen leg which appears after injury when the skin is broken. Infection enters the lymphatic system, causing a good deal of inflammation. This impairs the removal of excess fluids from the leg causing swelling. In severe cases an ulcer may appear, from which fluid may erupt. Can be treated with antibiotics and anti-inflammatory drugs combined with cold hosing to reduce swelling. **Call the vet.**

Digestive Disorders

Choke This is when a piece of food such as carrot or apple gets stuck in the gullet. The horse will appear very distressed, releasing vast amounts of saliva from its nostrils and mouth and will no longer be able to eat or drink. On examination, the obstruction can often be seen. Try to dislodge it with gentle massage and if this doesn't work, **call the vet.**

Colic This is a loose term used whenever a horse has abdominal pain. It is a common condition but can be potentially lethal. Among its many causes are: sudden changes to the diet or unsuitable food; exercise too soon after feeding; worm infestation; indigestion due to defective teeth (the horse cannot chew properly). Any of these can result in stoppage of the intestines or, in extreme cases, a twisted gut. This can prove fatal unless there is immediate surgical intervention.

Colic can be prevented by feeding regularly at the same times each day. Change diet gradually, worm regularly and have teeth checked often.

It the horse is to have a good chance of recovery it is vital to recognize the early stages. It will stop eating and may keep glancing towards its flanks. Patches of sweat may appear over the body and the horse may stamp its front feet, paw the ground and kick out at its belly with the hind-legs. Then, as the pain intensifies it will attempt to roll. Try to prevent this by gently walking the horse without exhausting it. Otherwise, try to provide as much comfort in the stable as possible. If symptoms appear to be subsiding, a small bran mash can be fed.
Call the vet.

Diarrhoea Obvious signs of diarrhoea are loose faeces ranging from very soft to liquid. If the problem persists, the horse will start to loose vital nutrients quicker that it can take them in, leading to dramatic weight loss. While looseness of the bowel can be quite natural, caused by rich grass, stress or excitement, it may have more sinister connotations, indicating worm infestation, salmonella or a bacterial infection. If symptoms persist, **call the vet.**

Skin Disorders

It is important that you check your horse's skin on a regular basis and a good time to do this is when you are grooming him. Skin problems are often hard to detect, especially in winter when the coat is thick. Once a problem is identified, treat immediately, or if you are unsure, **call the vet.**

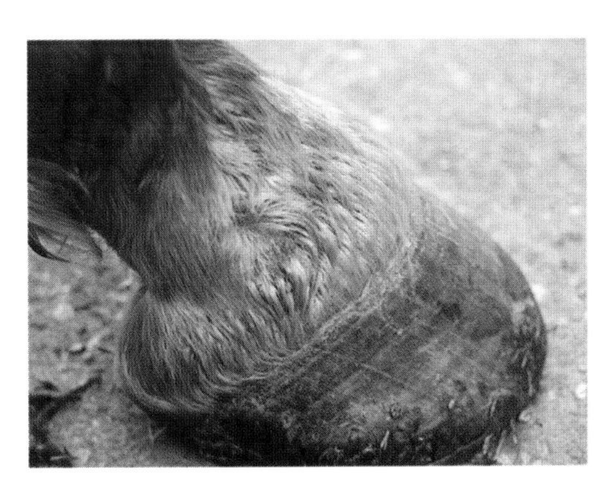

◀ Mud fever and cracked heels usually occur in winter when the paddock is cold and wet under foot. It can occur, however, in summer, as a result of an allergy.

▶ Sweet itch is an allergy to midges and is most common in ponies. Various lotions and shampoos can alleviate it, though the best remedy is to keep the animal stabled mornings and evenings when midges are at their most active.

▶ Occasionally a wound may take some time to heal. Usually a fibrous tissue called proud flesh will form, which will be permanent if not surgically removed.

Cracked heels and mud fever This is a painful winter condition when the skin on the legs, heels and belly becomes soft, or it can occur in summer when the skin is dry and cracked. This allows a bacterial infection to build up under the skin, causing it to ooze and large scabs to form. This can be treated by softening the scabs with an antiseptic shampoo before removing them. Treat the infected areas with an antibiotic cream. The condition can be prevented by keeping the skin clean and dry. For horses with higher susceptibility to this condition it is a good idea to apply an antibacterial barrier cream to protect the skin. If there is any doubt, **call the vet.**

Galls and saddle sores These are lesions caused by ill-fitting or dirty tack. The skin becomes raw and inflamed. Do not ride the horse until the cause is established and rectified and until the wounds are completely healed.

Lice Occurring mostly in winter, evidence of lice infestation reveals itself in large bald patches which appear where the horse has been rubbing itself to relieve itching caused by the lice biting. Treat with a preparation specially formulated for the condition and make sure to treat any other horses which have been in contact, whether they show signs of infestation or not.

Mange This has much the same symptoms as lice infestation, though it is usually confined to the lower leg. A tiny mite inflicts intense itching, causing the horse to stamp and worry at his legs. **Call the vet.**

Rain scald Prevalent in cold, rainy weather, this is caused by the same organism that leads to cracked heels and mud fever and can be similarly treated. Chapping appears over the upper part of the body and can be prevented by turning the horse out in a rug.

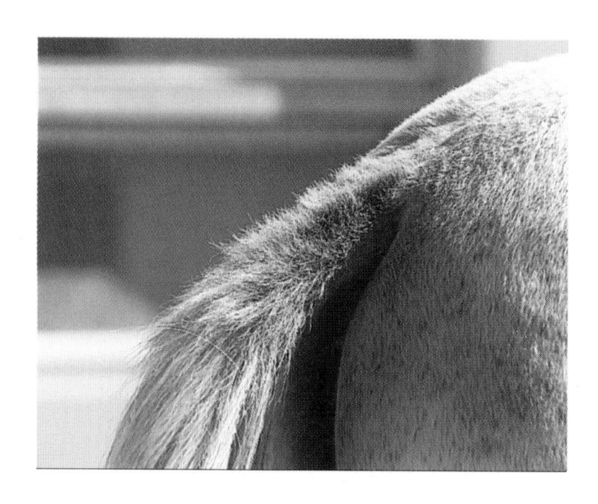

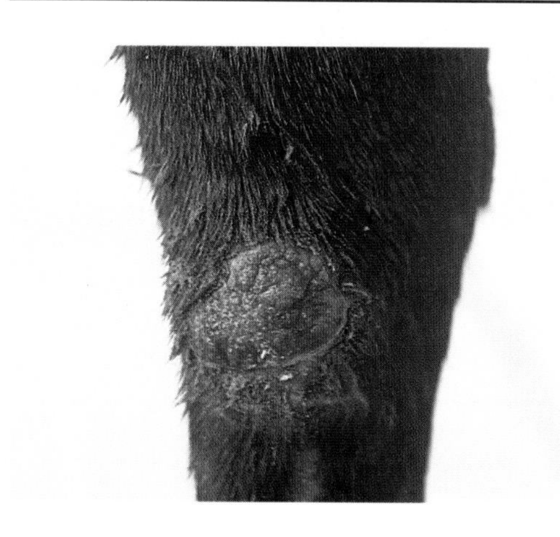

Ringworm This is a fungal infection causing circular bald patches with raised crusts to form on the skin. It is highly contagious and the horse must be immediately isolated, together with its tack, as the disease can be readily transmitted to humans and other animals. **Call the vet.** After following the vet's instructions regarding treatment, and when evidence of the infection has passed, thoroughly disinfect anything with which the horse has been in contact: ringworm spores can persist for many years.

Sweet itch This is caused by an allergic reaction to biting midges and is therefore more common in warm weather. The horse rubs its mane and tail against whatever is available, causing raw, oozing patches and even removing hair from the skin. Can be prevented by keeping the horse stabled

▲ Horses at grass are particularly susceptible to worms. Worm damage can be extremely harmful, making a regular worming programme essential.

mornings and evenings when midges are most active. Regularly apply fly repellents and special shampoos, even when the horse is stabled, paying particular attention to affected areas. Covering the entire neck and body with sheets is useful in severe cases.

Warbles These are large flies resembling bees which lay sticky eggs at the bases of hairs. The larvae hatch and burrow into the skin, eventually migrating to the skin of the back area. They cause small swellings with air-holes. If undamaged, maggots emerge in about a month and fall to the ground to pupate. After this has occurred, treat lesions as for open wounds. If an abscess forms, or the warble lingers beneath the skin, **call the vet as surgery may be required**.

Worms

It is vital that your horse is wormed on a regular basis. Worms left unchecked can cause discomfort, loss of condition, colic, permanent internal damage to the vital organs and even death. There are many worming products available; however, there is not one single one which will kill all worms. It is for this reason that you must establish a worming programme, alternating between products. If you are in a yard where there are other horses, make sure that they are all wormed on the same day and that the correct dosage is followed.

Pasture must be carefully managed. As well as weakening harmful weeds, regular grass cutting or 'topping' will help prevent the horse from eating worm larvae which crawl to the tops of stems. Rotating horses' grazing is also helpful and has the effect of depriving the larvae of their hosts, thus interrupting their life-cycle.

Wild horses do not suffer to the same degree from worm infestation as they are able to roam over large areas. This means that they are rarely re-infected and are less likely to develop a harmful build-up of worms in the body.

The life-cycle of worms The larvae are eaten by grazing horses, entering their digestive systems and shedding their skins several times before developing into worms. These lay their eggs in the horse's body which are expelled with the droppings. The droppings eventually disperse, allowing the eggs to hatch into larvae which are once again eaten by horses.

Bots These are the larvae of the bot fly which bears some resemblance to a bee. It lays its eggs on the horse's legs and the hatching eggs cause such irritation that the horse tries to lick them off. They enter the stomach where they develop into tiny grubs, attaching themselves to the stomach's lining and causing digestive problems and even ulcers. They are eventually expelled in the droppings when the adult fly emerges, beginning the cycle afresh. Bots should be carefully removed from the horse's legs, using a blunt knife, in an attempt to interrupt the cycle before it progresses further.

Lungworm (*Dictyocaulus*) These live most of their lives in the horse's lungs where they irritate the bronchial tubes causing coughing when the larvae are carried up the windpipe and are then swallowed. The eggs are passed out in the droppings. Lungworm is most common in donkeys and horses can easily pick up the parasite if allowed to graze on the same pasture.

Pinworm (*Oxyuris*) These live in the large intestine and lay their eggs just inside the horse's anus where they cause intense irritation.

Large redworm (*Strongyles*) The blood-sucking worms thrive in the horse's intestine, causing digestive problems. They can also migrate to blood vessels and organs causing considerable restriction of the circulation to major organs. The eggs are expelled in the droppings onto pasture and are hatched into larvae where they are again swallowed by horses.

Whiteworm (*Ascarids)* Common in very young horses, they can grow to a very large size and cause blockage of the bowel. Adult worms live in the intestines, laying their eggs which are passed out onto pasture together with the horse's droppings. Immature worms live part of their life-cycle in the lungs and cause coughing, nasal discharge and more serious damage. Once the horse is over a year old it tends to become immune.

Tapeworm (*Anoplocephala)* The worms are flat and ribbon-like in shape, being composed of segments, the last of which contain the eggs of the new generation. They live between the small intestine and the caecum where they can cause impaction, leading to colic.

Leg Disorders and Lameness

Considering how fine and slender they are, a horse's legs take an enormous amount of weight. During work, tendons and bones are under constant pressure. Strained tendons and ligaments are a common occurrence, as well as self-inflicted wounds caused by brushing and overreaching. Much lameness can be avoided with common sense. Don't overwork an unfit horse and use protective equipment such as overreach-, brushing- and tendon-boots. Take care when riding over rough or uneven ground and avoid prolonged trotting on hard surfaces, such as roads.

Broken knee This refers to broken skin on the knee rather than a fracture. It usually occurs when the horse stumbles and lands on his knees. If your horse is

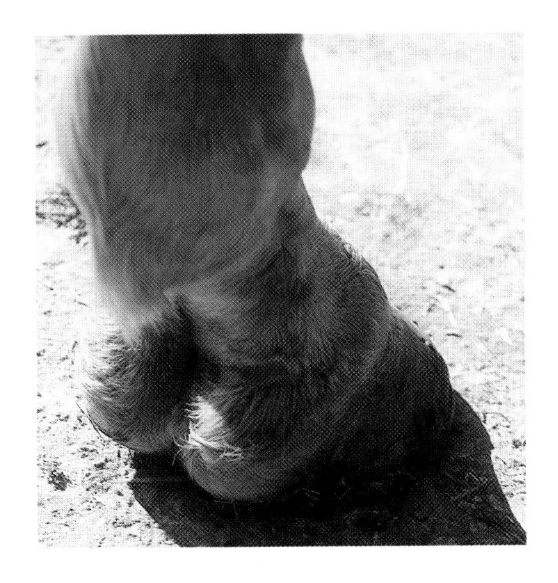

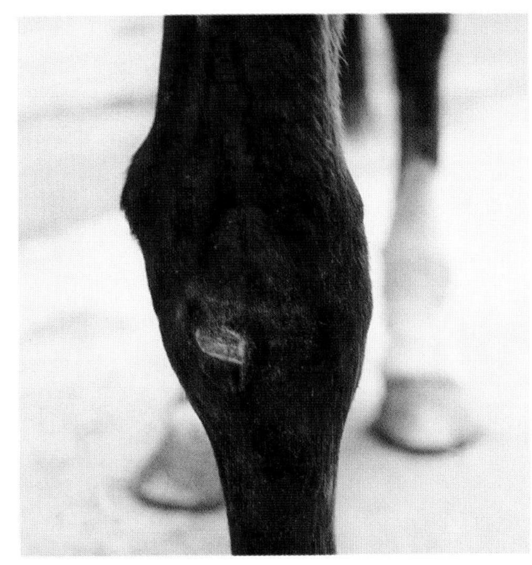

◀ Two common injuries which can occur when the horse is being ridden. An overreach (left) is caused by the hind foot striking the fore. Overreach boots will protect the horse from such an injury. Broken knees (right) are caused when a horse falls, causing the skin to break and, in severe cases, the joint capsule to be exposed. Knee-boots should be worn when hacking on roads or uneven ground. Both are potentially serious injuries.

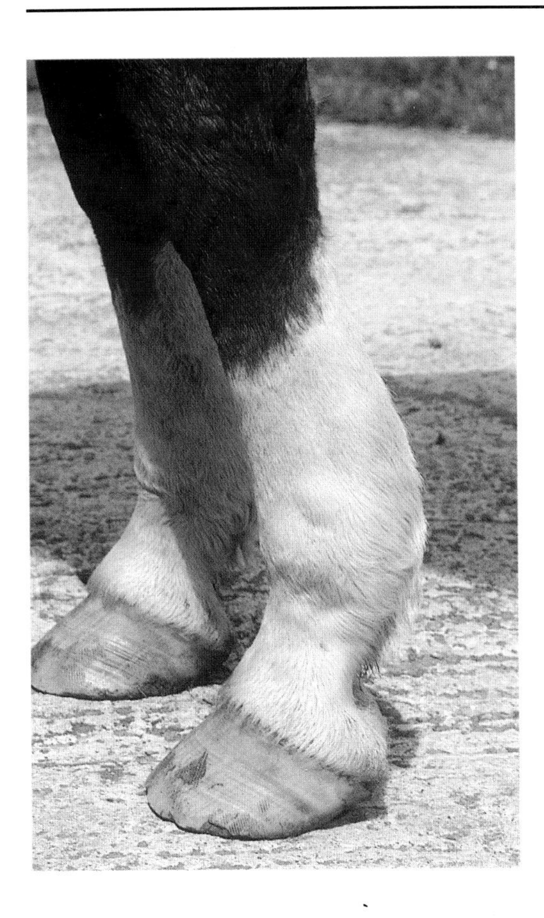

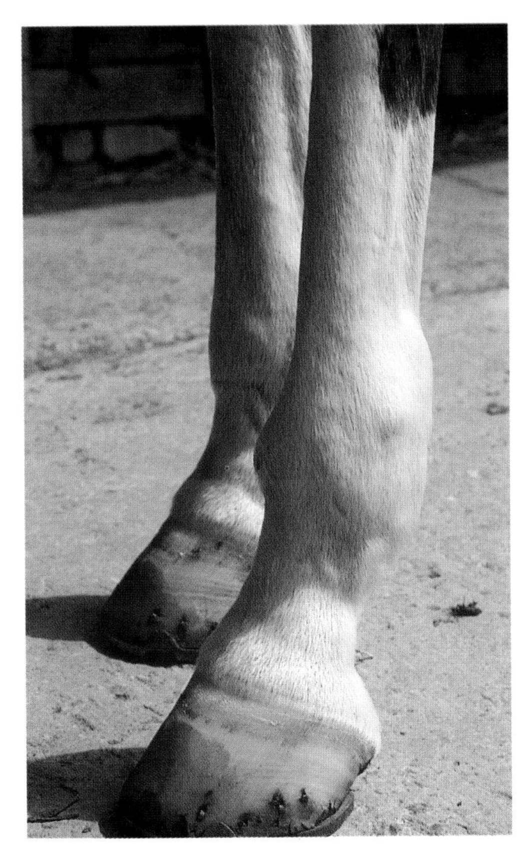

◀ On the left is the result of an old tendon injury. The horse's front tendons have collapsed, causing acute lameness and extreme pain. As the tendons have healed, they have become thickened and it will be impossible to ride it again as the tendons are now permanently weakened.

Windgalls (right) are harmless swellings above the fetlock, they usually swell up when the horse is resting after work. They rarely cause lameness, but are a sign of wear and tear.

prone to stumbling, equip him with knee-boots for his protection.

Self-inflicted injuries Most of these occur when the horse strikes one leg against the other and some of these injuries can be quite serious and cause prolonged lameness. Overreaching is when the horse strikes the heel or pastern of the front leg with his hind. Because the horse is shod this can inflict considerable damage and in severe cases cause a broken bone or severed tendon. Wearing overreach-boots will help prevent this injury. Other injuries of this kind are striking

▶ Laminitis is a painful condition, usually caused by excessive feeding, often on a surfeit of spring grass. The pain causes the horse to stand on his heels in an attempt to deflect weight from the painful toe area. The ridges and deformed shape of these feet is typical of a horse with laminitis.

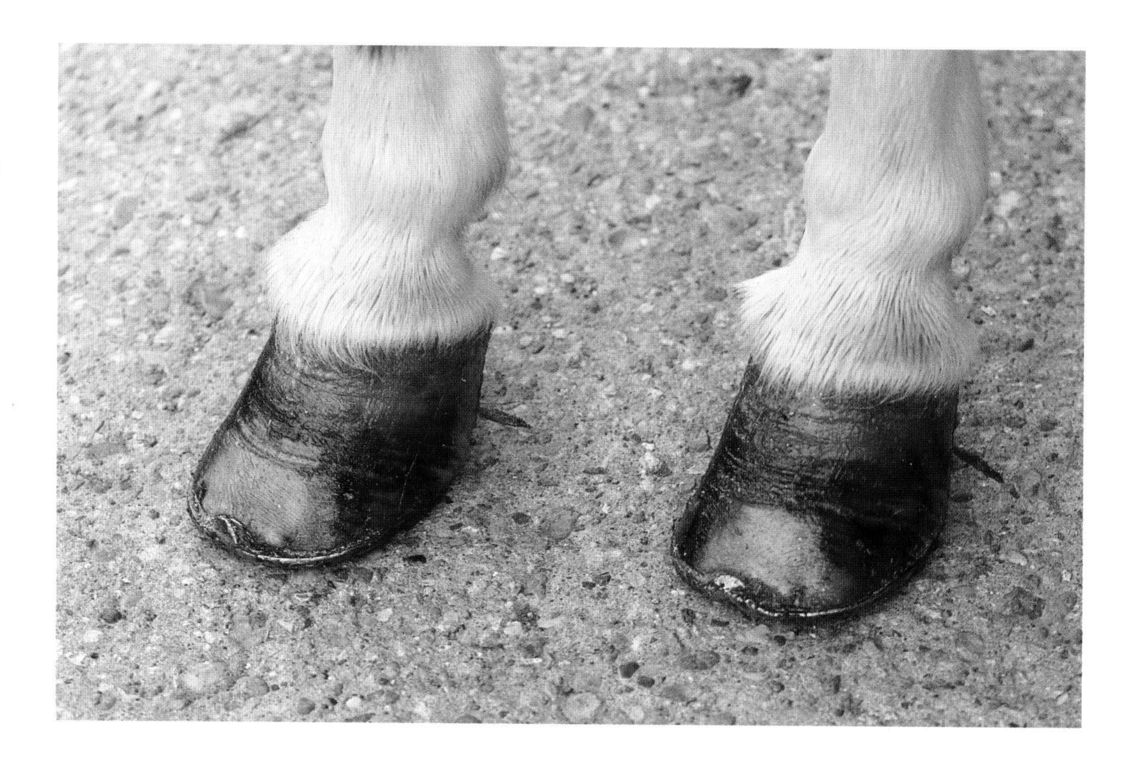

▼ Any swelling to the legs caused by a strain or tendon injury should be hosed with cold water for as long as possible. This hose-boot is ideal for the purpose.

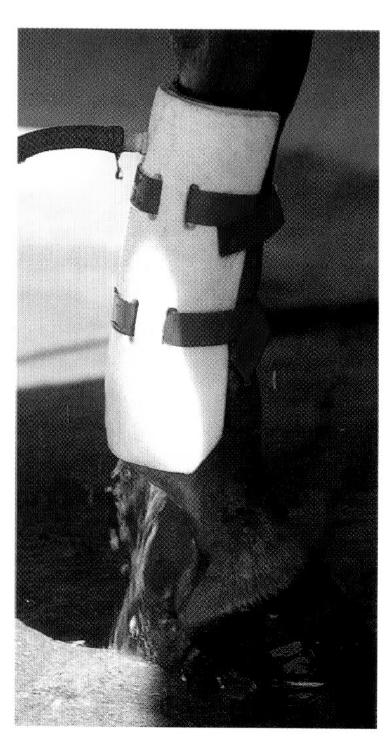

(which is further up and can also sever the tendon), and treading (which is damage to the coronet when the horse or another horse treads on it). This injury is common when travelling and care must be taken to protect the coronet by bandaging. Brushing is probably the most common injury and is caused when the fetlock joints rub together during exercise. Brushing-boots should always be used when schooling or if the horse's legs have a tendency to move close together.

Tendon injuries Horses are susceptible to strains and sprains. When these occur, the tendon will feel hot and swollen. The horse will be in severe pain, often unable to put the foot down, and in extreme cases will be said to have 'broken down'. The tendon will require at least 6 months to heal, with complete box rest in the early stages. Both the damaged and opposite legs should be bandaged to offer support. Sometimes the tendon is left permanently weakened with a 'bowed' tendon which is a permanent swelling. Care should be taken when working a horse who has suffered a tendon injury as a recurrence is more likely.

Bone lameness A **splint** is the most common type of bone lameness. It is caused when a small bony growth is formed on the side of the cannon- or splint-bone. A swelling and heat will occur while it is forming and often the horse will be lame for a while; but it is in general a trivial ailment. **Sore shins** are also a condition likely to cause lameness. They are common in young immature horses who are new to work. Repeated work puts too much pressure on the young fore cannon-bones causing pain, some swelling and heat. Other causes of lameness are **arthritis** or degenerative joint disease (**DJD**) due to wear and tear, such as **ringbone**, which is an enlargement of the pastern bones or of the coronet and **sidebone,** which is a growth on the cartilage near the heel. Another is a **spavin** – a swelling involving the small bones of the hock and **sesamoiditis** which is a swelling of the sesamoid bone behind the fetlock joint. (*See diagram p. 37.*)

Bursal swellings These are soft swellings, usually caused by wear and tear or strain. **Windgalls** occur above the fetlock at the side of the leg. They often swell up more during rest but do not usually cause lameness. A **thoroughpin** can be caused by bad conformation. It is a soft swelling between the hock and the tendon. **Capped hock** and **capped elbow** are painless swellings and do not usually cause lameness. They are an injury caused when insufficient bedding is used, causing the horse's joints to rub on hard ground. (*See diagram p. 37.*)

Foot disorders The horse's foot is most complex. It absorbs the shock of both horse and rider's entire weight, and has to be tough enough to carry the horse over rough terrain and hard ground. It is also the site of about 90 per cent of all lameness. In fact, this is the first place you should look when a horse becomes lame.

Keeping your horse's feet healthy is a prime responsibility. By picking out the feet at least twice a day and making sure that any sharp stones are removed, you can check that no damage has been done. A thorough washing with a disinfectant once or twice a week is also a good idea. Get the horse shod every 4–6 weeks and make sure that he is not given too much feed for the amount of exercise he does as this could cause laminitis. Don't let him trot on roads for prolonged periods. If you suddenly suspect lameness, dismount at once and check the foot.

Bruised or punctured sole These injuries are caused by treading on a sharp stone. Keep the horse stabled and rested until the bruise has subsided and the horse is sound. Don't be tempted to turn him out before he is sound as this will worsen the injury and it will take longer to heal. Once the foot is punctured, it is likely to become infected and develop an abscess when the horse will become very lame and unable to put foot to ground. The puncture hole will need to be enlarged to allow pus to escape and it will require poulticing to draw residual pus away. Antibiotics are more than likely to be required. **Call the vet.**

Corns This is bruising of the sole in the region below the heel of the foot. They are usually caused by leaving shoes on for too long. The horse will suffer increasing lameness which is more noticeable on hard or uneven ground and the horn is often discoloured by the presence of blood. The condition can be cured with corrective shoeing.

Laminitis This is an inflammation of the *laminae* inside the foot and is most common in ponies but occasionally horses. Because the swelling is contained, it is excruciatingly painful. It is caused by overeating, too much rich grass, lack of exercise or a release of toxins which cause a chemical reaction in the blood, causing constriction of the small blood vessels of the *laminae*. **Consult your vet**, but first try to ascertain the cause, which will help him with his diagnosis and treatment. Painkillers may be prescribed which will also help reduce swelling and corrective shoeing is another option. Once a horse has had laminitis it is likely to recur unless his diet is carefully

Capped hock is a bursal swelling caused when a horse, uncushioned by sufficient bedding, lies on hard ground. The swelling can be quite marked, but is usually painless.

monitored. Keep him off rich grass and avoid high-protein feed. Take special care of the feet and look out for any signs of discomfort.

Navicular syndrome This is usually caused by wear and tear and poor shoeing, and can be aggravated by poor circulation. It can also be hereditary. The condition involves damage to the navicular bone, the deep flexor tendon, and the surrounding tissues in the heel. The horse is sporadically lame, and may have an uneven gait and stumble easily. The condition can be readily diagnosed by x-ray. In the old days, a horse with navicular disease usually ended up being destroyed. However, with corrective shoeing, drugs to stimulate circulation, and even surgery, most horses can be restored to soundness. **Call the vet.**

Pedal ostitis This is similar to navicular syndrome, but the damage is to the pedal or sesamoid bones. **Call the vet.**

Seedy toe This is aggravated by a long toe and weak horn which pulls open the white line allowing access to infection. The foot is very painful when the infected area is tapped, and a black, semi-solid pus is produced. All the infected horn must be removed to allow healthy regrowth. The disease can be prevented with regular shoeing and foot hygiene, keeping the feet well picked out. **Call the vet.**

Sand crack Is a vertical crack which travels from the coronet to the toe. It can be caused by injury to the coronary band which impairs horn production: it is difficult to cure. If the crack is deep, infection may enter, causing lameness. There are remedies which your vet will recommend and careful shoeing will also help. **Grass crack** is a similar condition though it starts at the toe and travels towards the coronet. It should be treated in the same way as sand crack. **Call the vet.**

Thrush is usually caused by standing in a damp stable and is common in horses taking prolonged box rest. It can be avoided by keeping the stable clean and thoroughly cleaning and disinfecting the feet daily.

Thrush This is basically 'foot rot'. It usually starts in the cleft of the frog which becomes black and moist and develops a foul smell. It is caused when the horse has been left to stand in a dirty stable or muddy conditions for a prolonged period. The infected horn must be removed and the horn kept clean. An antibacterial spray or a weak solution of hydrogen peroxide will help prevent the condition from spreading. Only in very severe cases should the horse become lame. **Call the vet.**

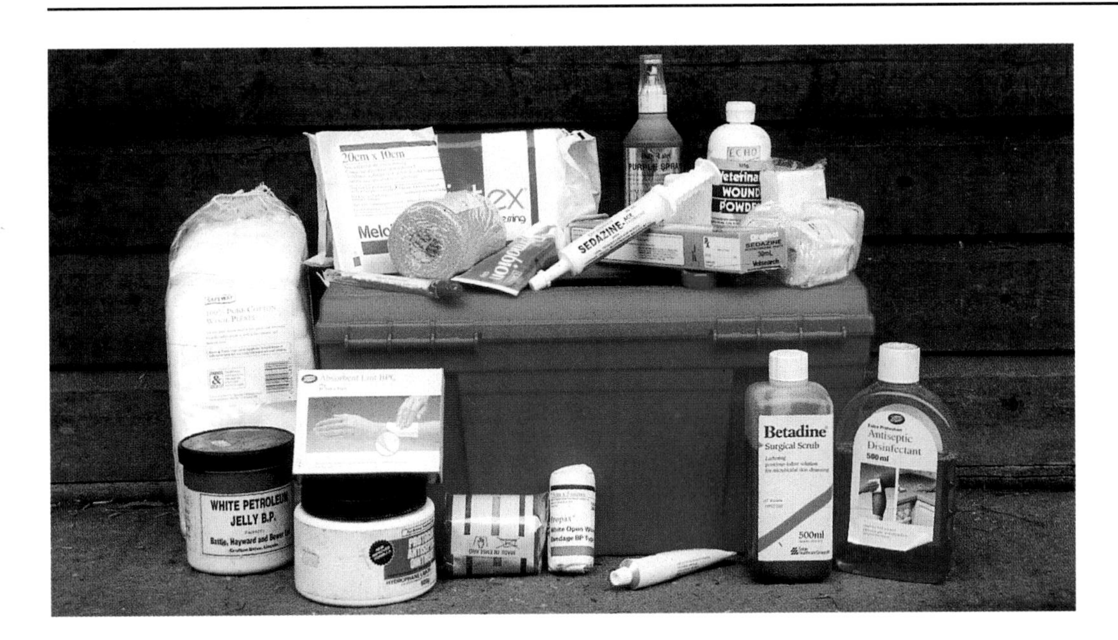

◀ Everyone caring for horses should have access to a first aid kit as infections can set in very quickly and cause lasting damage. When injury occurs, call the vet. Meanwhile clean any wound as thoroughly as possible; iodine-based scrubs are good for this purpose as well as simple salt water. Once the wound site is clean, treat with an antiseptic cream or wound powder. If the injury is severe call the vet.

Strains and tendon injuries should be hosed and bandaged, on the advice of your vet.

BONE LAMENESS AND BURSAL SWELLINGS

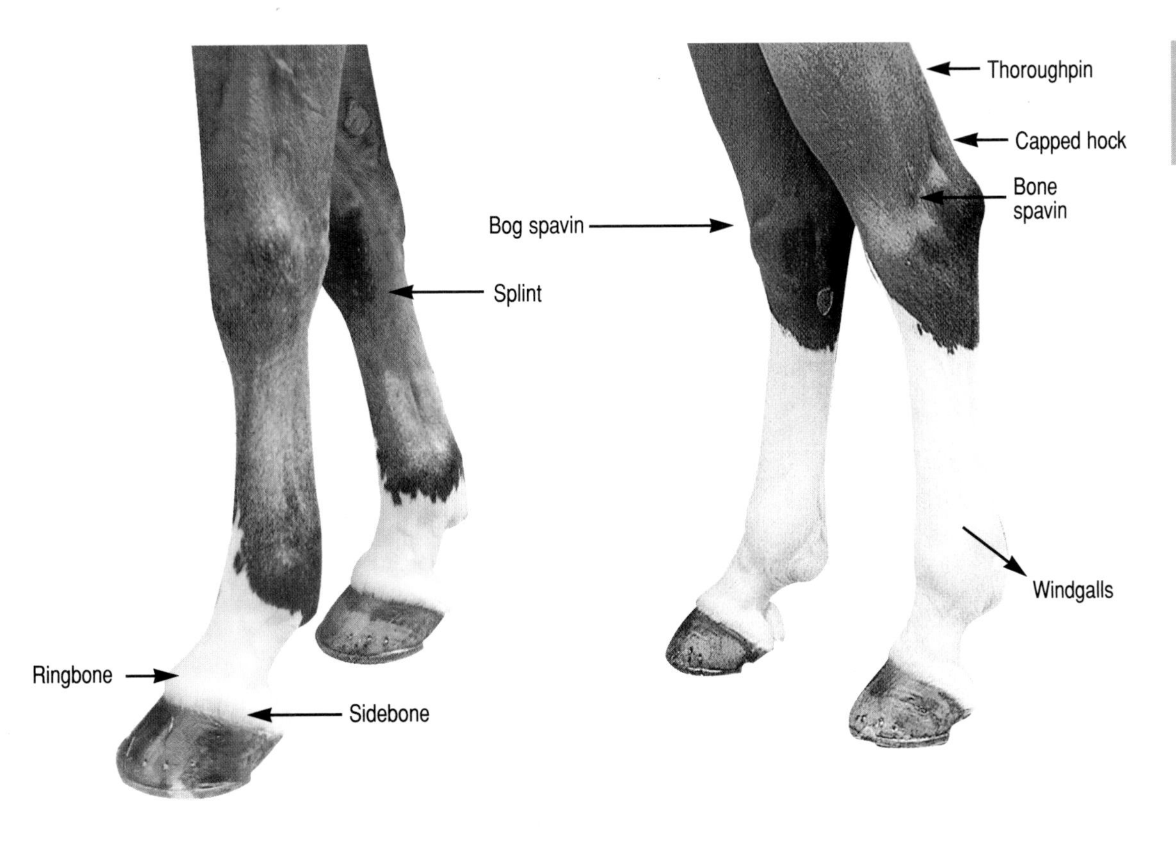

THE FOOT AND SHOEING

▼ Learn to recognize the various parts of the horse's lower leg and foot. Caring for your horse's feet is extremely important as they are subject to a huge amount of stress and are the most common seat of lameness. Pick the feet out at least twice a day and after exercise. Check that all loose dirt and stones are removed and that nothing is left sticking into the sole or frog. It is also a good idea to wash the feet once a week in a mild disinfectant which will reduce the risk of thrush occurring.

It is vital that your horse is shod regularly every 4–6 weeks. Failure to do this could lead to long-term and even permanent damage.

The horse in its natural state is a grazing animal, not designed to travel great distances at speed for a sustained amount of time except when fleeing from predators. When the horse was domesticated, it was immediately apparent that it would be unable to do the amount of work expected of it without protective shoes. The standard horseshoe has changed very little for centuries, only better, stronger irons and subtle shaping distinguishes a shoe made 100 years ago to one made today. However, new shoes have been developed to help correct foot problems, such as the egg-bar for weak heels or navicular syndrome, to a new lightweight shoe which can be glued onto a foot with weak horn that cannot hold a new shoe.

The farrier's job has changed also. Gone are the days of taking your horse to the village blacksmith. Today's farriers are highly trained individuals, likely to know as much about your horse's feet as your veterinary surgeon and corrective shoeing now plays an important part in the horse's well-being.

Many diseases of the foot, including lameness, can be avoided with regular and correct shoeing. Your horse should be shod every 4–6 weeks, depending on growth of horn. Although expensive, never be tempted to save money by delaying shoeing: even if the shoes aren't worn, the foot will still require trimming and the shoes may have become tight, causing corns and discomfort; letting the feet get too long will throw the foot out of balance, causing stress to the tendons and bones of the pastern and leg.

The farrier is highly skilled and qualified to do his job. Never try to shoe a horse yourself, or even to replace a nail, as you could do severe damage to the structure of the foot.

Check that your horse's shoes are in good shape and are still well-fitting whenever you pick the feet out: they could be loose, unevenly worn, a nail may be missing or the shoe may have become twisted. Summon the farrier at once to correct the problem, as a loose shoe coming off may cause a great deal

THE LOWER LIMB, HOOF AND SOLE

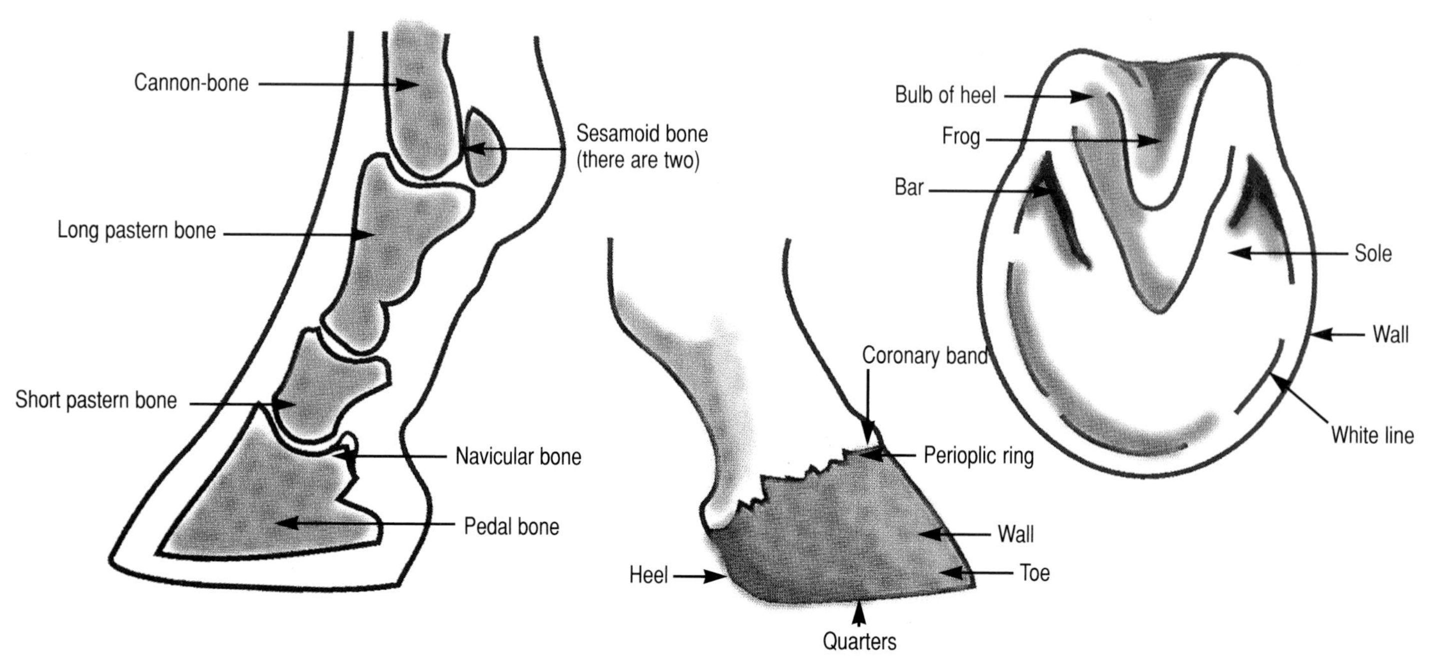

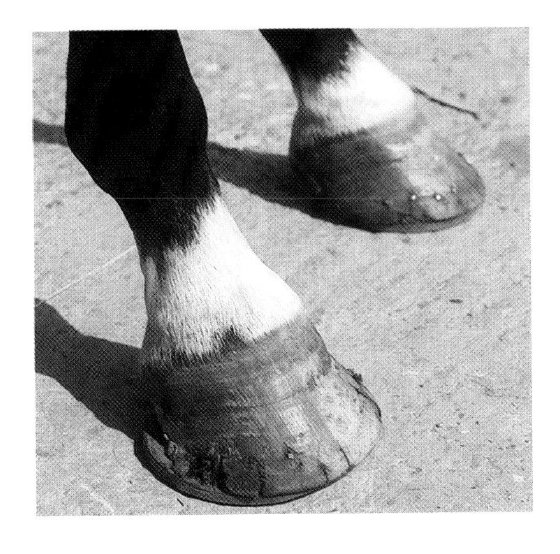

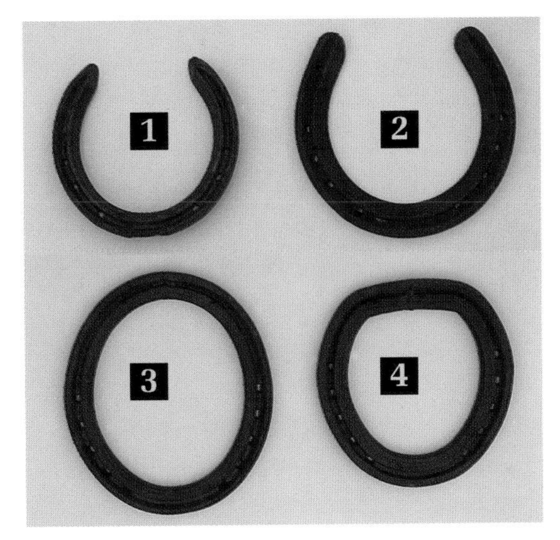

Pictured left is an example of a horse which has been left for far too long without a visit from the farrier. The loose shoe is actually skewed and could cause considerable damage if not immediately removed.

Pictured right are some examples of different shoes:
1 Hunter, 2 Wide-web, 3 Egg-bar, 4 Straight-bar.

A visit to a forge is virtually a thing of the past, and many modern farriers have mobile forges which run on bottled gas. This has made cold-shoeing almost obsolete, hot-shoeing, in any case, being far superior. Your farrier will build up a good relationship with your horse, becoming quickly aware of any special requirements needed and ensuring that his charge's feet are kept in good shape and a healthy condition.

The Farrier's Tools.
Buffer – Used with a hammer for knocking up the clenches when the shoe is removed.
Clenching tongs – Used for making clenches, by pulling over the nail-ends.
Drawing knife – For paring and trimming the hoof.
Hammer – For hammering in nails and clips.
Hoof-cutter – For cutting the hoof wall.
Nail-puller – For removing nails.
Pincers – For removing a shoe.
Pritchel – For carrying a hot shoe.
Rasp – For removing horn and tidying the hoof at the end of shoeing.

of damage. It is possible to knock back a risen clench using a hammer.

Methods of shoeing There are two types of shoeing, 'hot' and 'cold'. Cold-shoeing is the least effective as the shoe cannot be properly shaped to the foot. Moreover, with the invention of the mobile forge it has virtually become a thing of the past.

Hot-shoeing is by far the best method as the shoe can be shaped to fit the horse's foot exactly, with no overhang liable to cause injury. Because the shoe is burned onto the hoof, any imperfections such as raised areas which could cause the shoe to sit incorrectly become apparent, enabling the farrier to make adjustments. Shoes come in different types and sizes to suit each horse and the type of work expected of him.

The most common is the fullered shoe, fullering being a groove which is hollowed out of the centre to make it lighter and offer more grip. These come in two widths, the **hunter** shoe – which is the most widely used – and the **wide-web**. This is usually used on heavier horses or those with sensitive feet. Other shoes such as the **egg-bar** or **straight-bar**, are reserved for corrective shoeing, usually at the suggestion of a veterinary surgeon.

For horses likely to be often ridden on hard roads, it is a good idea to have a road nail fitted on each shoe. These have a hard tungsten tip which remains raised, offering extra grip. Good grip when competing is most important: ask your farrier to fit shoes with stud-holes when studs can be screwed in and tightened with a spanner. (Used only on soft ground.)

Removing a shoe yourself should be carried out only in an emergency if the loose shoe is likely to cause damage. In most cases it is better to call a farrier,

Removing the front shoe The farrier holds the foot in position between his knees so that his hands are free. Using a hammer and buffer, he knocks the clenches up. Next, using the pincers, he places its jaws between the shoe and the hoof, starting at the heel. Using a jerky action, he pulls towards the toe, easing the shoe loose: this is repeated on the other side until the shoe comes away. If the shoe fails to loosen easily, a pair of pliers is used to remove some of the nails. All this must be done quickly and calmly, making sure that the shoe, together with any nails, are properly removed before replacing the foot on the ground.

Removing the hind shoe Standing with his back to the horse's head, the farrier holds the leg up over his thigh, pressing his side against the horse's hock. This prevents the horse from kicking out. The hoof is allowed to rest on the inside of the farrier's knee. He would never, however, attempt to hold a hind-leg between his knees – this is extremely dangerous. The shoe is removed in the same way as the front.

most of whom will respond to an emergency promptly. However, it is a good skill to know yourself. Get your farrier to teach you the technique and ask him to watch you practise it a few times.

HOW TO HOT SHOE

1 The farrier removes all the old shoes and will usually take them away for recycling. Next he cleans up each foot and removes any loose or uneven horn to enable him to assess each foot.

2 Using hoof cutters, he trims away the wall in order to bring the hoof back to the same size as the last time the horse was shod. He will usually remove more of the toe than the heel as this grows quickest.

3 The foot is then rasped with a file to remove all loose horn and to even up the sole.

4 The farrier selects a shoe the correct size for the horse. It is placed in the furnace until it is red-hot. Holding the shoe in position, he then shapes it on an anvil to fit the horse.

5 When happy with the fit of the shoe, he holds it against the hoof; the burn-mark will reveal any unevenness in the rasping and confirm that the shoe is sitting properly and is correctly shaped to fit the foot.

6 Once correctly shaped, the shoe is cooled in water. Then it is nailed into place. There are eight nail-holes on a shoe – though not all are usually needed. Three on the inside and four on the outside are most commonly used.

7 Next the nail ends are twisted and bent over to form a clench using the clenching tongs. For this, the farrier will usually rest the hoof on a metal tripod, making it easier to work.

8 The hoof is then finished off with a rasp when all the rough edges are smoothed off. Finally, all the clips (small pieces of metal which help to secure the shoe) are tapped into place so that they are flush with the hoof.

The end result will be a shoe which is symmetrical, with no overlapping hoof. The clenches should be in a straight line and not penetrate old holes and the clips should be neatly fitted against the side of the hoof. Inside, the shoe must be fitted up to the heel for protection. The frog and sole should be neatly trimmed, but not overtrimmed.

Handling your horse is the beginning of establishing a good relationship with him. Get to know him well and learn to understand his moods. Talk to him so that he learns to recognize the sound of your voice and hold out your hand so that he knows your smell. Always approach him head-on, but slightly to the side, talking to him gently to warn him of your arrival before giving him a reassuring pat.

How to put a headcollar on

If you wish to catch your horse with a headcollar while he is in the stable, move to the near side of his head and gently slip a rope around his neck to form a loop. This will give you control if he decides to move back. Next, hold the headcollar on both sides and slip it over his nose then, using your right hand, flick the strap up and over his head and secure the buckle. If the horse tries to move off or throw his head up during this exercise, go with him so that he can't get away; he will gradually learn to keep still during the entire procedure.

Make sure that the headcollar fits correctly and that it is neither too tight nor loose. The noseband should be halfway between the eye and the muzzle and you should be able to insert three fingers between it and the horse. It is not a good idea to leave a headcollar on in the stable or field which could be a hazard if caught up.

When tying a horse up, never tie him straight to a ring; make a loop with bale twine which will break if the horse panics (*see p.44*). Always tie with a quick-release knot, which is again easy to undo if the horse panics. Don't leave him tied up indefinitely – he will become stiff, cold and bored: do whatever job is required, then put him back in his stable or turn him out.

Approach at the near side of the horse's head. Slip the lead rope under and over the head. Have the headcollar unfastened and ready.

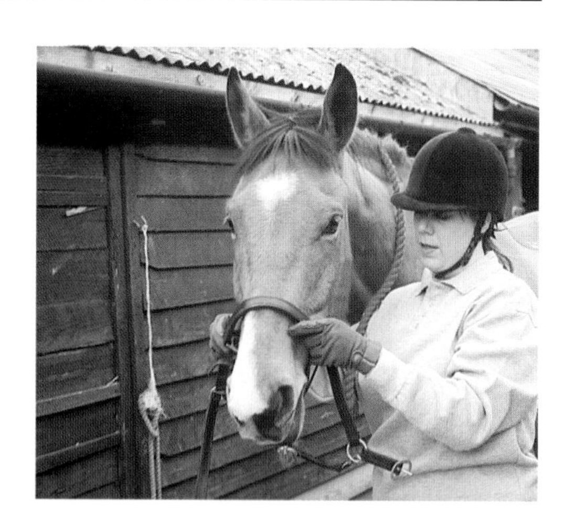

Still holding the rope, stand with your back to the horse's rear and gently slip the noseband of the headcollar over his nose.

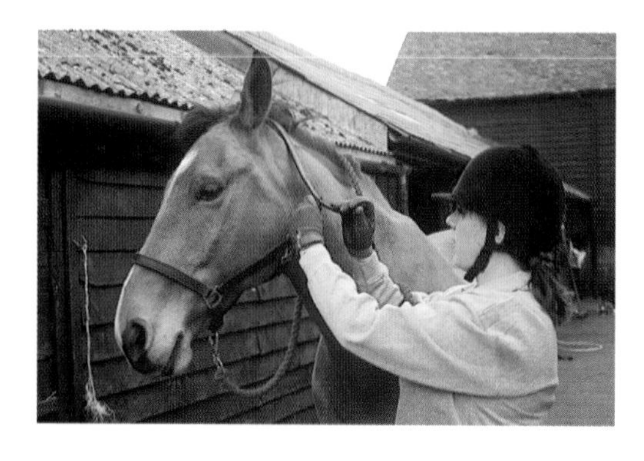

Quietly pass the end of the headcollar over the horse's head and fasten.

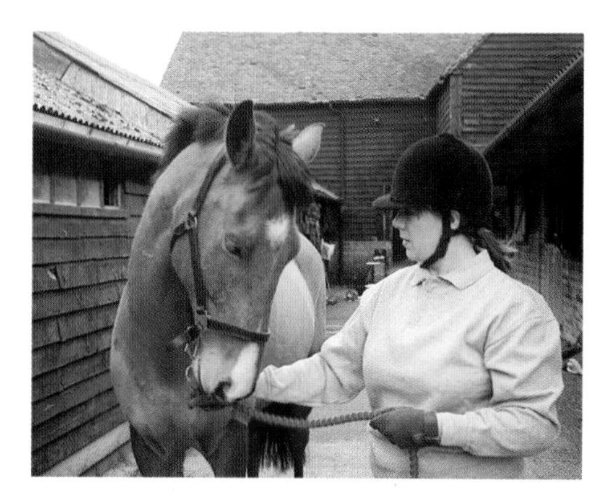

Give him a pat and lead him away. If your are inexperienced with horses, first try putting a headcollar on a calm and placid horse in a confined space.

When catching a horse in a stable, encourage him to come to you and stay near the entrance. Don't get yourself in a situation where you risk being kicked.

Leading a horse in-hand

Every horse should be taught to be well behaved when led. A headcollar is fine for this purpose while in the stableyard. It is usual to walk on the horse's near side as the majority of people are right-handed which means that your strongest controlling arm is nearest the horse. Your right hand should be about 12 inches (30cm) from his headcollar, with your left hand holding the end. Never ever loop the rope around your hand: it could be severely damaged and you could even be dragged along if the horse were to bolt suddenly. Don't pull a horse around sharply; a horse cannot turn quickly and his legs could be injured in the process. Nudge him around gently, all the time keeping yourself on the outside.

Leading a horse on the road

When leading a horse on the road, more restraint will be required. Always lead him in a bridle, wearing gloves and a hard hat. Walk in the same direction as the traffic, placing yourself on the inside. Hold the reins the same way you would hold a rope and, once again, don't wrap them around your hand. If the horse starts to play up, give him a short, sharp jerk to make him behave. Practise getting him used to traffic by standing him by the side of the road, but at a safe distance from it. Gradually introduce him to the road when it is quiet, in order to slowly build up his confidence. It is vital that a horse becomes accustomed to traffic as one which is traffic-shy is a danger to both rider and motorist.

▲ The more you handle and get to know your horse, using gentleness, tact and a quietly encouraging voice, the more confidence will develop between you.

All horses have different personalities; so beware when handling a new horse for the first time. Anti-social behaviour such as biting, kicking and barging, should be anticipated well in advance.

Other forms of restraint There are times in your horse's life when he needs to be restrained, perhaps because he requires veterinary treatment, clipping, or worming. If a horse discovers something is unpleasant, his natural reaction is to run away and sometimes a firm hand isn't enough. Simply distracting him with food will often do the trick or lifting up a front leg will stop him moving away. If more control is required, put his bridle on – a lunge cavesson is also useful. If all else fails you can resort to twitching. A metal twitch is preferable: fitted tightly to the nose it appears to reduce the horse to a trance-like state, making him oblivious of the very thing which frightens him. The process is thought to cause the release of endorphins, a natural painkiller, into the bloodstream, producing a calming effect. Sometimes, however, even this is not enough and you can ask your vet to administer a mild sedative.

▲ Leading a horse on public thoroughfares calls for great care and attention. Most motorists would not understand a horse's reaction and very few will slow down for you. Take precautions: always lead your horse in a bridle for extra control, and wear bright colours or a fluorescent tabard to make yourself as conspicuous as possible. Always lead the horse in the same direction as the traffic, yourself on the inside.

► When tying a horse to a metal ring (above right), the lead rope should be passed through a loop of baling string which, being weaker, would more easily break should a horse panic. It is safer for a horse to break free rather than damaging itself by struggling. For the same reason use the quick-release knot illustrated here when tying up.

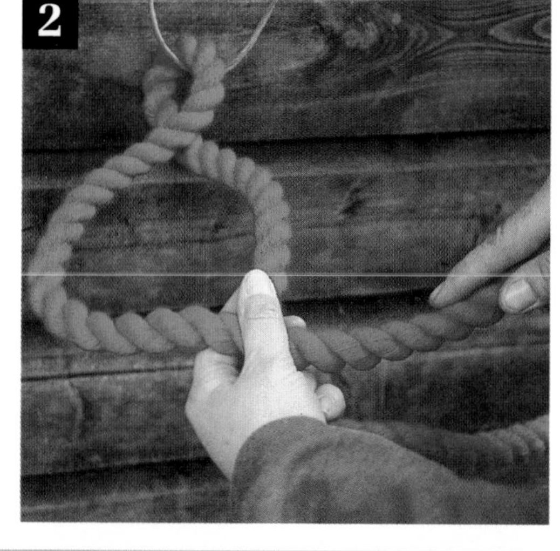

TYING A QUICK RELEASE KNOT

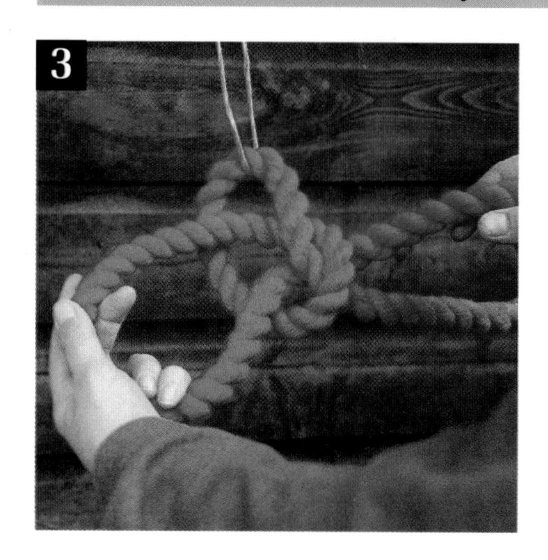

◀ This well designed stable yard is perfect for handling horses. Completely enclosed, there is a central tying-up area, with plenty of room for people to pass and no dangerous tools left lying around.

Care should be taken not to crowd tied-up horses together and handlers should always give horses' hindquarters a wide berth. Even the most placid of horses can kick out without warning.

▶ This horse is content in his stable. There is plenty of room for him to move about, he has a haynet from which to feed at will, and there is plenty of fresh water on hand. Removing droppings (skepping out) at regular invervals throughout the day will make mucking out easier, as well as keeping your horse's environment very much fresher.

He will also require mucking out thoroughly once a day and his water checked regularly.

Remember that stabled horses require at least one hour's exercise each day, and preferably twice a day. Without regular exercise, horses can become prone to stable vices, such as windsucking, cribbing and weaving.

A well-designed stable yard, with a sensible layout and good facilities, will enable the yard manager or horse-owner to care for his horses with ease and in safety. There are some essential factors which should be considered when planning a yard.

The stables should be situated in rows or around an adequately-sized courtyard. The stables should be airy, but free from draughts. Good natural light is always a bonus. Larger yards often have an isolation stable for sick horses, well away from the main yard.

As with all electrical fittings situated outside, a circuit-breaker, installed within the main fuse box of the electricity supply will reduce injury should electrical wires become wet or damaged.

In winter, flooded stables are far from ideal, wasting bedding and causing discomfort to horses. Good drainage and leak-proof stables are therefore essential.

With crime on the increase it pays to make the stable yard as secure as possible. Locked gates with sturdy latches will keep opportunists at bay, but in some locations it may be necessary to have either a person on the premises 24 hours a day or a closed-circuit TV system.

The tack-room must be the most secure area in the stable yard. Ideally it should be situated close to an occupied building and should be locked and alarmed, as the cumulative value of the contents of even one tack room may represent a great deal of money.

A good water supply with a hose attachment is important; ensure that there is a hook to safely coil the hose away after use.

Make sure there is a area safe for tying-up horses, ideally in an enclosed area well away from mucking-out tools and dangerous machinery.

◀ This well constructed stable yard, built at the turn of the century, fulfils all the requirements. It is brick-built and sited around a square. There is plenty of room in which to tie a horse up safely. It has plenty of drains, a good water supply and a securely locked tack-room. The stables are well aired, but draught-proof, making then warm in winter and cool in summer

The muck heap should be positioned well away from the stables to avoid odour and encouraging flies in summer, but should be near enough to allow easy access to the stables. Muck heaps can often be offensive to neighbours, so they should be placed as far away as possible from private dwellings and other people's property. The heap should be readily accessible to a muck removal truck.

The muck heap should be removed regularly by a specialized contractor who may charge a fee. Burning is an effective way of disposing of it but is not recommended for environmental reasons. Muck must not be used for fertilizing grazing land as this could encourage worm infestation of the soil to persist.

Storage areas and places where hay is kept are potential fire risks and should be sited well away from stables and the muck heap. These areas should be kept dry and it goes without saying that smoking should be prohibited.

◀ Wooden stables such as these are the most common. Available in kit form you can design your own stable yard relatively inexpensively. They aren't as resilient as brick-built stables and if not properly secured can blow down in strong winds.

Other options are stalls within a barn. While this system guarantees freedom from draughts, they can get very warm in summer. The stalls are usually separated by half partitions and bars which can make some horses uneasy, especially at feeding time. If you already have a barn, however, it is a good way of providing stabling.

▲ An adequate water supply is essential. Fitted with a hose, it will be easier on your back when filling water buckets and washing muddy hooves. However, make sure that the hose is safely coiled up when not in use.

Utensils

Wheelbarrow
Shovel
Four-pronged fork or pitch-fork (with blunted prongs)
Skep
Hose-pipe
Shavings fork
Rake
Broom

Fire extinguishers should be accessible to all parts of the yard. Advice should be sought from your local fire department regarding your yard's particular requirements.

Stable accessories such as securing rings are used for tying up horses and for attaching haynets. Care should be taken to choose the most appropriate positions at which to site them. Purpose-built mangers prevent horses tipping over their feed bowls and should be safely positioned, preferably boxed-in to prevent horses trapping their feet beneath them.

Hayracks positioned at the same height as you would a haynet are a useful alternative to a haynet. Do not position them too high above the horse's head as dust is likely to fall into its eyes.

Salt licks are a constantly available source of salt for the stabled horse. There are also various other mineral licks available.

Water bowls and bucket fittings come in an array of shapes and sizes and their suitability depends on the type of horse they are designed to accommodate.

Toys are available from various sources and are designed to alleviate boredom in a horse confined to stable.

Bedding

Mucking out a straw bed

Straw is the most popular form of bedding. It is relatively cheap, comfortable for the horse, and fairly easy to handle. However, it should not be used for horses will allergies to dust and fungal spores.

Stabled horses must be mucked out thoroughly in the morning and droppings removed (skepping out) at regular intervals during the day.

To muck out thoroughly, remove all droppings and wet straw from the bed. All the straw should be sifted thoroughly with a fork and piled up against one side of the stable. The floor should be swept clean before replacing

▶ When not in use, keep all mucking out utensils tidy and out of the reach of horses.

the straw. To prevent injury and draughts, the straw can be piled up in banks against the walls and new straw should be added daily to top up the bed. Try to keep the bed as clean and as deep as possible. This will be more economical in the long run and will ensure that the horse is kept as comfortable as possible. If the horse has a tendency to eat his bed, mix the new straw with old to make the bed less palatable.

Once a week, the straw should be piled up away from the floor and the stable floor disinfected and left to dry.

Wood shavings and paper beds
Both are alternatives to straw and are good for horses with allergies to dust and fungal spores, although horses can very occasionally become allergic to the ink on paper.

The bed must be kept as clean as possible and should be mucked out thoroughly once a day and the droppings removed at regular intervals throughout the day. The bed should be forked and fluffed up daily to prevent if from becoming impacted.

Auboise bed
This is a fairly new and entirely natural product made from the hemp plant. It is particularly absorbent and, like shavings, is suitable for horses with allergies. It is expensive to start the bed off, but gets more economical as time goes on.

▲ Water buckets should be sturdy with securely fixed handles. Feed bowls should be wide enough for the horse to eat comfortably. These have covers to keep food clean and away from flies.

▼ Two of the most common forms of bedding are shavings (left), ideal for horses with allergies. Straw (right) is the least expensive option.

A TYPICAL STABLE ROUTINE

7.00am

1 Check horse over to make sure no injuries have occurred during the night and that he remains in good health.
2 Put on horse's headcollar and tie him up.
3 Pick out feet and adjust rugs, as necessary.
4 Muck stable out and put a bed down for the day.
5 Give horse a haynet and his first feed of the day.
6 Remove headcollar.

9.00am

1 Tie horse up. Remove droppings from stable.
2 Give a short grooming, tack horse up and exercise him.

10.30am (Or on return from exercise.)

1 Untack the horse
2 Give a thorough grooming, making sure feet are picked out and shoes are in good condition.
3 Put on day rugs.
4 Give haynet.
5 Remove headcollar.

12.00pm

1 Tie up.
2 Check water.
3 Remove droppings.
4 Give second feed.
5 Clean tack.

2.00pm

Turn horse out in a paddock, if available.

4.30pm

1 Bring horse in from field.
2 Groom off mud.
3 Pick out feet.
4 Give haynet.
5 Give third feed.
6 Remove headcollar.

8.00pm

1 Tie up.
2 Remove droppings.
3 Check rugs.
4 Top-up water, if necessary.
5 Refill haynet, if necessary.
6 Give fourth feed.
6 Remove headcollar.

▶ Ensure your stable yard is kept safe and tidy at all times. Don't leave jumps lying around or in the manège as they can be dangerous to a loose horse.

▶ (Opposite) Peace personified – all mucked out, fed and watered and the yard tidy and swept.

HORSES AT GRASS

Keeping a horse at grass is as close as he is likely to get to his natural environment and a horse grazing in a lush green field on a summer's day is an idyllic scene. However, it is not an option to be undertaken lightly. In fact, grass-kept horses require as much monitoring as a stabled horse.

Many horses prefer to be kept at grass; they may well fret if left in a stable or suffer from allergies, making an outdoor environment more desirable. Ponies, in particular, thrive at grass and even a Thoroughbred, with a good shelter, rugs and supplementary feeding can settle down well. Mares and foals are also much happier at grass and youngsters are far less likely to pick up stable vices, such as cribbing, windsucking, and weaving if left out. However, many countries have severe winters, and wintering horses out in extreme conditions is not advised.

Before you decide to turn your horse out, much thought and preparation is required and many factors need careful consideration. Is there enough grazing to support your horse? Remember a horse living out all year round requires at least 1 acre (0.4 hectares) of pasture and if grass is poor, supplementary feeding. In addition, there must be a constant water supply and the paddock must be well fenced.

Grazing

The quality of grass is very important to the grass-kept horse. One paddock is rarely enough: two would be ideal, as one can be rested, rolled, topped and fertilized while the other is in use. This also breaks the worm cycle, reducing infestation. If it is not possible to have two or more paddocks, electric fencing

▼ Doing what comes naturally. This pony is contentedly grazing in the summer sunshine. Grass makes coats glossy and eyes bright. Don't let your horse over-graze, however, as laminitis and colic are both serious disorders likely to be caused by over-eating.

Most horses love to roll, which is especially exasperating in winter as it will be your job to remove the mud from his coat. However, it is an important part of the horse's natural life and something which they appear to enjoy immensely. Watch out for excessive rolling, however, as it could be a sign that something is amiss; the horse may have lice or be suffering from colic.

can be used to section off parts of the paddock in rotation in order to rest the grass. All droppings should be regularly removed and checks should be made that no rubbish has been deposited or has blown into the field.

A keen eye should be kept on weeds, many of which are extremely harmful to horses and should be dug up and burnt. Learn to recognize the poisonous ones (*p. 56*) and deal with them immediately. Too many weeds will gradually smother grass, so careful management is vital.

Note that too much rich grass can be a problem, particularly for ponies and 'good doers'. Overeating causes major problems, such as colic and laminitis. Sectioning off paddocks will go some way to discouraging the horse from eating too much.

In winter there is very little nourishment in grass, and what is available is sparse, so you must be prepared to put plenty of hay in the field and give short feed as required.

An example of a poor paddock. It has been over-grazed and weeds such as dock and ragwort have been allowed to proliferate. A good rest, fertilization, topping and rolling is what is needed to restore it to a suitable condition for grazing.

Horses must never be left in the vicinity of a fence such as this, which consists of a rusty old metal gate and barbed wire. This is most unsuitable, highly dangerous to any animal, and should be avoided at all costs.

Post and rail fencing is the most expensive, but requires little maintenance and is totally safe for horses. Treating the wood beforehand will deter horses from chewing it.

▲ A dense hedge is one of the most aesthetically pleasing types of barrier and if well maintained will offer a source of shade and shelter.

▶ Make sure that field gates are padlocked securely to deter thieves and discourage unwelcome visitors.

▶ Place water troughs away from overhanging trees and with plenty of room around them to prevent horses from becoming trapped. Galvanized metal troughs with a self-filling device are ideal; however, you should still check them once a day and make sure they are regularly cleaned out.

Fencing and Gates

Adequate fencing is a primary concern when turning a horse out. It should be of the best quality and in good condition, and regular checks and repairs should be made, with particular attention to outer boundaries.

Fencing ranges considerably in price and you will obviously get what you pay for. Wooden post and rail and its synthetic equivalent is the most expensive but safest for horses. Next in preference comes natural hedging, which is asthetically pleasing but should be well maintained and reinforced with electric fencing. Less suitable is post and wire which is lacking in strength and if allowed to become slack can cause injury. Barbed and sheep wire should be avoided at all cost as they can cause serious injury.

Good gates are also important; they should be large enough to give both you and your horse comfortable access. They should swing open smoothly and have secure fasteners together with a chain and padlock for security.

Water Supply

It is vital that the horse at grass has a constant supply of fresh water. A galvanized metal trough fitted with a ball-cock is the perfect solution; however, it should be monitored and cleaned out regularly. Other less ideal options are containers, which must be checked, cleaned and refilled daily, or a natural stream could be used. Its source, however, should be regularly checked for contamination. Do not allow horses to drink from streams which run through farmland as they are likely to contain chemicals. Fence off all stagnant and unsafe water.

Shelter

Whether natural or manufactured, adequate shelter is essential. In summer, horses need to shelter from the heat of

Horses living out all year round should have some form of protection from the elements. This purpose-built shelter is ideal.

the sun and from flies, while in winter a windbreak and somewhere to get out of the rain is vital.

Only the hardiest of native ponies are able to survive winter without a rug. Make sure that if you use a New Zealand it is fully waterproofed, well fitting and undamaged. Check and adjust it twice daily and have a spare in case of damage.

In severe weather an under-rug is recommended; it is also possible to buy hoods which cover a horse's head and neck for further protection against the elements. (*See p. 78 et seq.*)

Never turn out a horse alone; horses are herd animals; without company they are likely to be miserable, and even attempt to jump out of the field. When introducing a new horse to a group, do it gradually and keep a vigilant watch that it is being accepted.

Care of the Horse at Grass

Horses living out require just as much care and attention as those which are stabled. They should be visited twice daily, caught and checked over for injuries. Any mud should be removed, but don't over-groom; removing the coat's natural oils will destroy an important barrier against cold and rain. Pick out feet and have them shod regularly.

Refit any rugs and feed as necessary. Do not single out one horse to feed in the field – it may cause companions to become jealous and steal his food, resulting in fighting and injury.

Horses living out all year round can be exercised but cannot be brought to the highest level of fitness. In summer, they are prone to obesity and in winter their thick coats will hamper them during fast work.

Security

It cannot be overstated that security is extremely important, and more so for horses living out permanently. Unscrupulous people may steal horses from fields, causing anguish and heartbreak to owners. Take precautions – choose a field where your horse can be monitored, either by the field's owner or yourself. Fit the gate with

Freeze-marking is a painless process. It is an excellent way of ensuring your horse's security. It can be expensive, but the cost may well be reduced if you can organize a group booking when several horses can all be treated at the same time.

good quality padlocks and keep the key with you, rather than hidden by the gate.

Have your horse freeze-marked; this is a painless procedure and will ensure that a stolen horse can be traced.

The horse's personal number is entered into a database along with the owner's details and the horse cannot be offered for sale without the owner's authority.

Some of the many plants poisonous to horses. Other dangerous plants not shown are: white campion, horsetail, acorns, deadly nightshade, woody nightshade, meadow saffron, monkshood, water dropwort, black bryony, bracken and rhododendron.

Learn to familiarize yourself with them and remove and burn them before turning horses out to pasture. Fields should be checked on a regular basis for regrowth.

The Combined System

This is the most common and preferable arrangement for most people. It means that the horse is stabled at night in winter and turned out during the day to stretch its legs. In summer, if the weather is good, the horse can live out all the time; however, in the heat of summer when flies are particularly irksome, many people keep their horses in during the day and turn them out at night when it is cooler. It also helps to control the grass-fed horse's weight, which can easily increase when lush spring grass begins to appear.

It also enables you to keep your horse fit while giving him freedom to roam as he chooses. This will relax him and make him more amenable when it comes to work.

◀ This horse has a thick winter coat, allowing him to keep warm even in cold, wet conditions. Horses wintering out should be monitored regularly and given adequate shelter; in very cold weather a New Zealand rug should be provided for extra protection.

▲ A correctly balanced diet is vital to your horse's well-being. You should try to get him to drink prior to feeding. Feed bowls should be wide enough for the horse to eat comfortably and the water bucket should be sturdy.

Feeding your horse the correct amount of food for his weight, type of work, and personality, is quite a science. There are a multitude of different feeds on the market and learning to use them correctly can be quite baffling for a beginner. Even before buying feed, get some advice. If there was a previous owner, ask them, or ask an experienced person to help you. Feeding the wrong type of food can seriously harm your horse, making him far too spirited to handle, or adversely affecting his general condition.

Feed can be split into two categories, the first being roughage or bulk which is the mainstay of the horse's diet. This consists of grass, hay, or hay substitutes, such as haylage. However, because the horse finds these quite difficult to digest, he is unlikely to get sufficient energy from them to do any kind of work. Consequently, they need to be supplemented with concentrated feed, e.g. oats, maize and barley. These are much more easily digested and contain higher levels of protein for energy. Not all animals require concentrates, however; some native breeds can live quite happily on hay and grass alone and horses not in work can remain healthy on good-quality hay.

How to work out your horse's weight

Knowing your horse's weight is useful when determining how much to feed him. You could take him to a weighbridge which would be ideal; however, these are hard to find. The next best thing is a weigh-tape which will give you a rough estimate, or you can use an ordinary tape measure. Measure the horse around the girth area, then the length from the point of the shoulder to the buttock. Using these measurements calculate the horse's weight using this formula:

Girth^2 inches x length in inches divided by 300 = weight in pounds.

(For kilograms multiply pounds by 0.45.)

Rules of Feeding

- Feed small amounts of concentrates at regular intervals.
- Allow access for most of the day to roughage, either grass or hay.
- Make sure that feed is of good quality and has not become stale.
- Try to encourage the horse to drink before feeding, but allow access to water at all times.
- Avoid letting him drink large amounts immediately after feeding or fast work.
- Feed by weight, not volume.
- Make changes to feed gradually.
- Do not disturb the horse while he is feeding.
- Do not exercise a horse for at least an hour after feeding.
- Feed a succulent food every day.
- Feed according to the amount of exercise done. Don't feed in anticipation of work you intend to do.

Types of concentrated feed

Barley The grains are shorter than those of oats and have very hard husks. It can be fed rolled, micronized (cooked in a microwave oven), flaked (heat-treated) or boiled. It cannot be fed whole when it is indigestible. It is less heating than oats and a little more fattening. Care should be taken when feeding barley as some horses are allergic to it, causing them to break out in a rash.

Coarse mix This can best be described as 'muesli' for horses. There are many different varieties and brands available which are composed of a mixture of grains, peas, beans, grass and additives. The fibre content varies according to type – usually high for non-heating meadow mix types, low for competition mixes. They are usually combined with molasses or glucose syrup, making them palatable and dust-free.

Cubes These consist of ingredients similar to those of coarse mix, compressed into pellets.

Cubes and mixes are formulated in entire ranges with different types to suit every kind of horse and level of activity. They have a distinct advantage in that they are nutritionally balanced and of consistent quality, as well as being easy to feed and store.

Maize Has the appearance of thick cornflakes and is sweet-smelling. It is

▼ A horse's diet should be assessed according to the amount of work it does. Its habitat and age should also be taken into consideration. Horses in light work should be fed a high roughage/bulk ratio and less concentrates. Horses in hard work will require more concentrated feed such as oats, barley and high-performance mixes. Remember, however, that highly concentrated feed should not be given to a horse on a rest day. If there are any doubts concerning your horse's diet, seek expert advice.

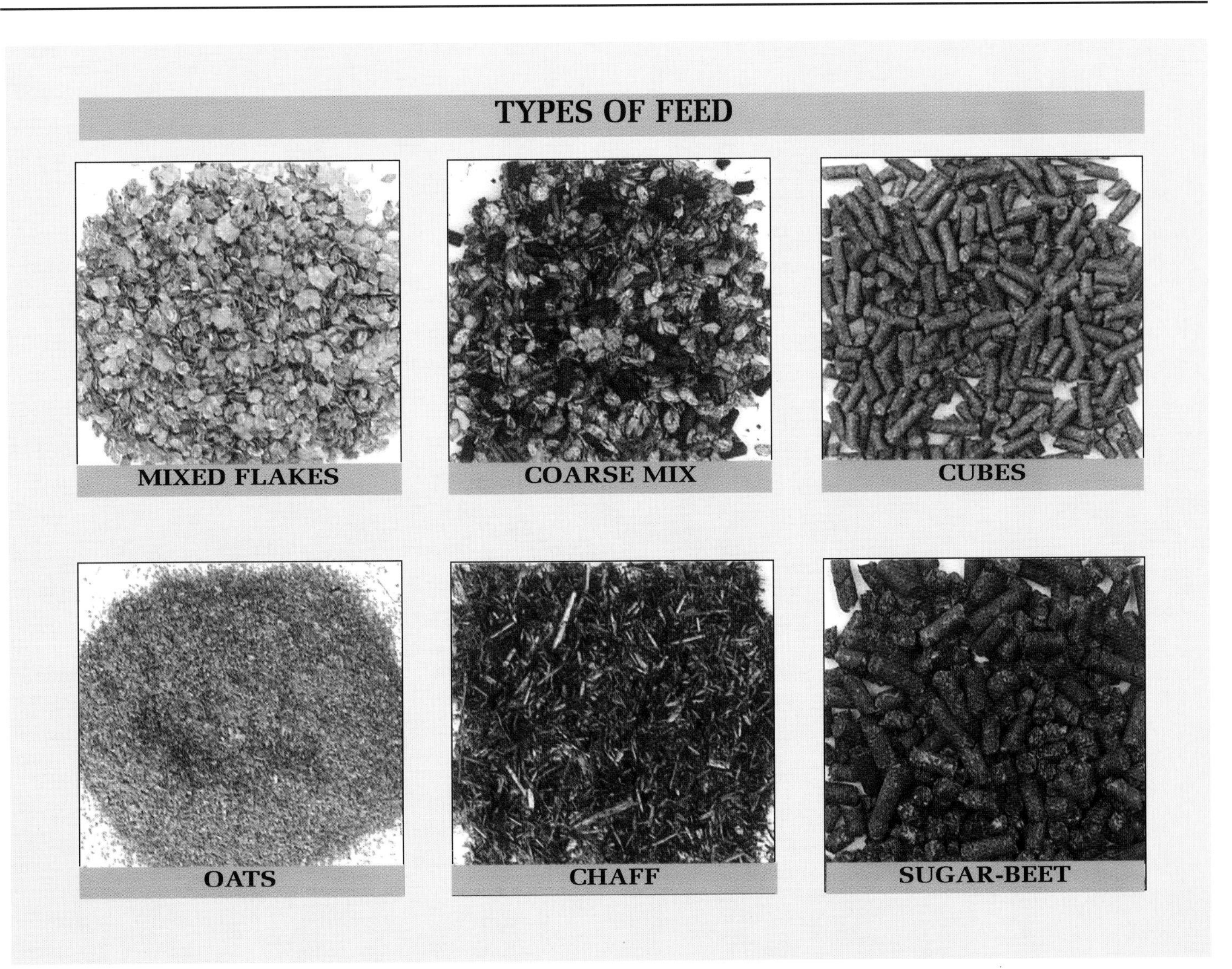

Feeding Example

This guide is based on a 16hh middle-weight horse, competing in riding club events in medium work, and stabled in winter.

Weight	500kg (1100lb)
Total feed	12.5kg (27½lb)
Hay	65% bulk 8.2kg (18lb)
Short feed	35% concentrates 4.3kg (9½lb) This could consist of oats, barley, alfalfa, chaff, sugar-beet and carrots, or a medium energy mix.

Feed amounts according to your horse's needs and the amount of work done.

What to feed?

Here is a formula to give you an idea of what to feed your horse. It is, however, only a general guide. Like people, horses vary in shape and metabolism. Watch your horse's weight carefully as he may require more or less to maintain perfect condition.

- Use a weigh-tape (or if you have access to one, a weighbridge) to determine your horse's weight.
- The average horse's daily food intake is the equivalent of 2½% of his body weight.
- The chart below is designed to give you a rough idea of the amount of food required for different sizes of horses and ponies.

Type & height	Approx Weight		Total Feed	
	kg	lb	kg	lb
13.2hh pony	255	560	6.3	14
14.2hh cob	400	880	10	22
15.2hh	450	990	11.25	25
16.3hh (Thoroughbred)	500	1100	12.5	27½
16.3 (Hunter type)	600	1320	15	33

1 kg = 2.2 lb (See concentrate to bulk chart below.)

high-energy with less fibre, so can be mixed with chaff or other grains. Useful for fattening and generating warmth it is, however, very heating, so feed sparingly. It usually appears in mixes.

Oats are considered ideal for feeding to horses. Whole oats should be plump, hard and shiny, and can be fed to horses in hard work; they are also suitable for horses in medium–hard work. Bruising or crushing makes them more digestible. Avoid oats that are dusty or appear to be all husks. Oats have a heating effect so are not usually suitable for ponies. Do not feed to horses who are resting.

Linseed This is the seed of the flax plant. Fattening, and with a high oil content, it is good for the coat. Feed 8oz (225g) dry weight 2–3 times a week. Good in a mash.

Preparation Care should be taken when

This chart will give an idea of how to split your horse's diet between bulk – which is hay, haylage and grass – and concentrated feed such as oats and barley. Generally, the harder the horse works the more concentrates are required and the bulk should be reduced accordingly.

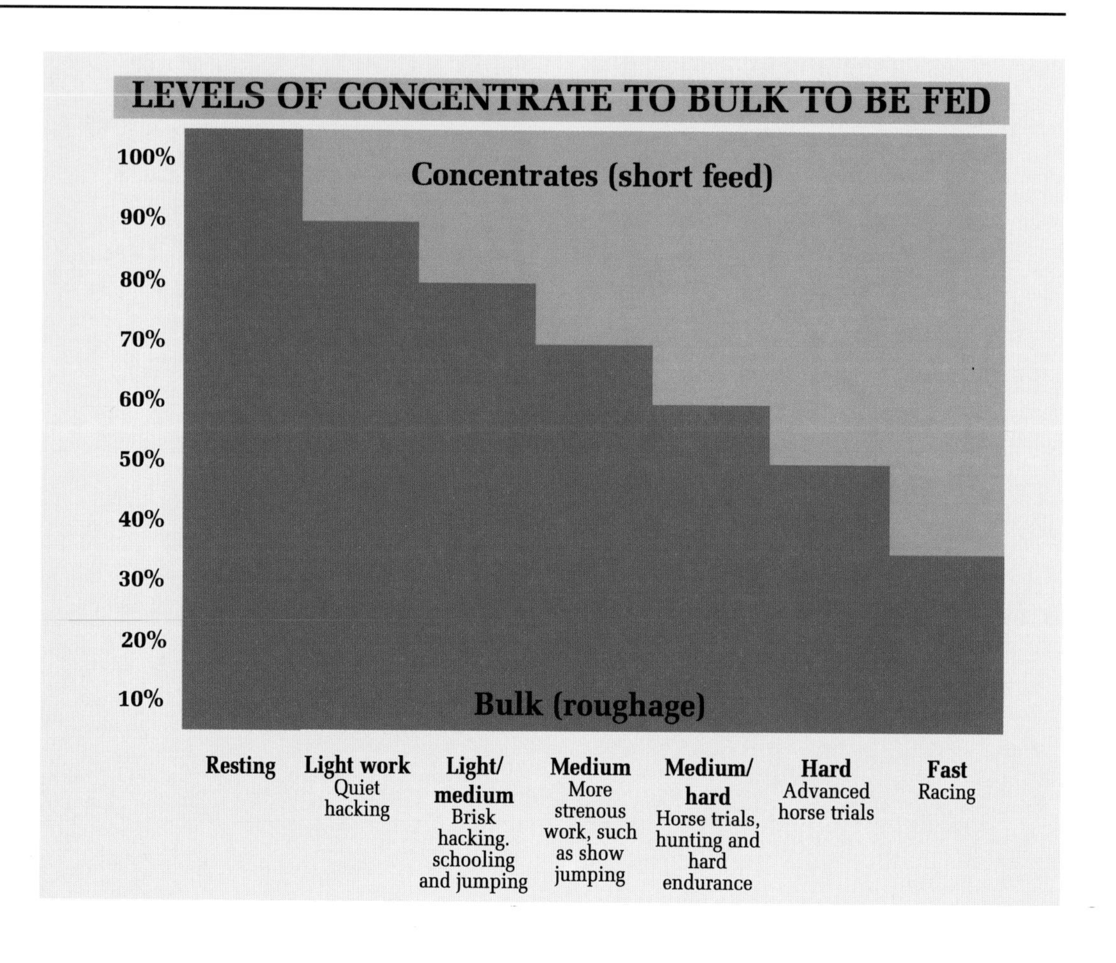

preparing a linseed mash as it is poisonous if not handled correctly. Soak linseed overnight in cold water, then bring it to the boil for at least 10 minutes before simmering until the seeds are soft. If mixed with a larger quantity of water it can be fed as a tea, with less it will be more like a jelly.

Sugar-beet Comes in pulp and cubes. It is high-energy and high-protein and very palatable. It must never be fed in its dry state, however, and should always be soaked for at least 24 hours before use.

How to make a bran mash

Bran is a low-energy feed consisting of the husks of wheat grains. It has little food value but is valuable as a laxative. It can be fed to ill or old horses as a mash when it will be soft and easy to eat. It should only be mixed with other feeds in very small quantities.

Put about 2–3lb (900–1350g) bran in a bucket. Pour boiling water over and stir. It should be wet but not too sloppy. Add some salt and possibly a handful of oats to taste. Place a sack over the bucket and let is steep until cool enough to feed. Add carrots, apples and supplements, if required, and serve.

Types of roughage

Roughage is the main source of fibre in a horse's diet and vital to the digestive process. Because of the length of the horse's colon it is possible to extract nutrition from it, and particularly from fresh grass and good-quality hay.

Grass is a natural source of roughage. Its nutritional value will vary through the seasons, and it is at its best in early summer. It contains all the protein and minerals a horse needs for a healthy life. However, because of seasonal fluctuations, supplementary feeds must be fed to all but the hardiest of breeds.

Hay is dried grass and comes in two types. **Meadow hay** is from permanent pasture and consists of a variety of grasses and herbs and is probably the most natural form of feed, other that grass. **Seed hay**, as its name suggests, has been especially sown from seed,

▼ Learn how to correctly tie a haynet. Thread the tie through the ring, loop it through the bottom of the haynet and tie with a quick-release knot, threading the loose end through the loop for added security. A haynet falling to the ground can make a horse panic if he were to get his feet caught in it, and cause serious injury. Don't ever leave empty haynets lying around on the ground in the stable yard; they are a danger to both horses and people.

▲ Mares in foal or with foals at foot have special feeding requirements, as do foals themselves. Consult your vet for dietary advice.

▶ The top show-jumper opposite is at the peak of fitness. He would have been fed a higher amount of concentrate than bulk to give him the extra energy for such strenuous activity.

treated as a crop to achieve a maximum yield. It is usually of better quality than meadow hay.

Hay forms a large part of the horse's diet and must therefore be of the best quality. Feeding dusty hay full of fungal spores can cause serious respiratory problems which can become chronic. If the hay is dusty, and there is no alternative but to feed it, it should be soaked for at least 2 hours, but no longer, as the nutrients it does possess will be washed away.

Haylage or vacuum-packed grass is more nutritious than ordinary hay. It is cut and left for only a short time and is then made into bales while still damp and covered in air-tight polythene when a cold fermentation takes place. It is ideal roughage for feeding to horses subject to respiratory problems as it is dust-free. The disadvantages are that if there are any holes in the polythene the haylage will turn sour; the bale must therefore be consumed within 4 days or less, if possible.

▶ Have your horse's teeth checked regularly, as problems in this area are often the main cause of weight loss. Here, the dentist is filing the rough edges off the horse's teeth, a process most horses don't seem to mind, or at least very soon become accustomed to.

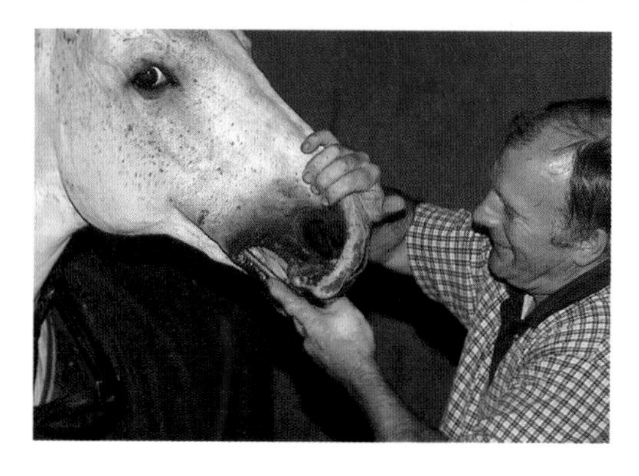

Silage This is the least common form of roughage. It is moist, and has a strong-smelling, acidic odour. It is grass which has been preserved by a hot fermentation process before being baled and wrapped in airtight polythene. Once opened, as haylage, it must be carefully wrapped and stored as it can easily spoil, causing problems if eaten.

Alfalfa This is highly nutritious, having high levels of protein and is also high in calcium and other minerals: it can be fed to resting or convalescing horses.

Chaff This helps improve digestion, encouraging horses to eat more slowly and chew more thoroughly. Add 1–3 double handfuls to the feed. Chaff is chopped hay, oat straw, alfalfa or dried grass. It is possible to process this yourself, with a chaff-cutter; however, there are many ready-prepared brands available, often mixed with molasses to make them more appetizing

Water Finally, make sure that your horse has access to water at all times. Check that his buckets are clean. Don't merely top them up – first empty them before refilling them with water.

Supplements

There are various types of supplements designed to be added to feed. There are times in your horse's life when some added vitamins may be required, particularly when old and ill or for mares and their foals. Other supplements can be given to improve the appearance of the coat and general condition or to improve horn growth.

There are other more natural supplements which can be fed to horses every day, such as carrots and apples. These make a tasty treat, cut lengthways into large pieces to prevent choking. Cod liver and corn oils are a rich source of energy and can add condition as well as improving the coat. Cod liver oil is also rich in vitamins. Other useful additives include minerals, salts, and garlic. It is very important to follow manufacturers instructions when feeding vitamins and minerals as over feeding can be dangerous.

FITNESS AND EXERCISE

▲ This horse is taking part in a three-day event and has to be at a peak of fitness to take part in this most strenuous of sports.

▶ Hacking out in open fields is a good form of exercise, as well as a pleasure for both horse and rider. However, get the landowner's permission first before encroaching on his property.

In their wild state, horses are accustomed to wandering and grazing at will. Once domesticated, maintaining them in surroundings similar to their natural environment will keep them content and in a state of equilibrium. However, keeping horses permanently at grass just isn't practical, especially if you wish to get your horse to a level of fitness needed for competition or even hacking. Grass-fed horses simply don't have the energy required and this is the reason why they are stabled, where their food intake can be carefully monitored and they can be exercised with a view to producing a horse with sufficient stamina for speed and endurance.

However, turning a horse out for a couple of hours a day will do wonders

for his mental health: horses who are permanently stabled may develop neuroses such as windsucking, cribbing and weaving. Some may even fret, all causing loss of condition. For these reasons it is vital that the stabled horse is exercised every day. If you cannot ride him on a particular day, he must be turned out to stretch his legs. There are other ways of exercising – lungeing is a good option, though should not be practised for too long as continuous trotting in a tight circle is very strenuous. Some yards are fitted with horse-walkers: this is a circular contraption with a motor which turns at walking pace and usually take four horses which are loosely tied up to a bar coming from the centre. The horse is then led by the moving bar, and is encouraged to walk forward. These are useful because they offer gentle exercise; however, it can be tedious for the horse. Make sure that you get him used to the horse-walker but don't forget that you have left him there.

If you have two horses, you can lead one and ride the other. This should only be attempted by an experienced rider and only if the horse is well behaved in traffic. Always lead him in a bridle, holding the reins or using a lead rein clipped to the outer bit and threaded through to your side. This will give you extra control if he misbehaves; never loop the reins around your hand and always keep the unridden horse between you and the traffic, going in the same direction and with his head about level with the ridden horse's shoulder.

When hacking out on public roads, make sure that you can be seen. There are many items of fluorescent clothing, from tabards to strips for the bridle and boots for a horse's legs. Never hack out in dark clothing and avoid riding at dusk or when it is dark. If you decide to ride a horse which has a full hunter clip, he will need to wear an exercise sheet to keep his loins warm.

When hacking, be particularly aware of road safety. Always tell another person where you are going and the length of time you intend to be away. If possible, avoid going out on your own. To maintain your horse's interest, don't take the same route every day. Cantering in the same place too often may teach him to bolt as he begins to anticipate your intentions.

When riding, always make sure that

▼ A walking hack on roads is an excellent way of getting your horse fit as it strengthens the muscles and tendons of the legs. If you do trot on hard roads, only do so uphill; this is beneficial to the horse without putting undue pressure on his front feet. It is a wise precaution to put knee-boots on your horse while riding on the roads.

Exercise on a lunge lead is a good way of getting horses fit. Build up gradually, as continuous work on a tight circle can cause strain to the legs.

you have the correct equipment for the job and that your horse has adequate protection; for example, a martingale for jumping, and brushing- and overreach-boots for protection from injury. Make sure that you are wearing the correct approved headgear and that you have sufficient body protection, particularly when jumping or engaged in fast work.

Fitness training

Horses in unfit condition are termed 'soft' and, like humans, can do very little exercise before feeling any ill-effects. Over-exertion may cause disorders such as colic, also tendon and muscle injuries may occur. It is a good idea to keep your horse reasonably fit, exercising him regularly and turning him out as often as possible.

However, some horses – specifically hunters and eventers – work very hard on a seasonal basis. When their work is finished they are rested for a period of time. This is called 'letting down' or 'roughing off'. The horse gradually has his feed and exercise reduced so that the effect on his system is gradual. He will then be turned out to grass to have his rest.

The opposite of 'letting down' is termed 'bringing up'. The horse is brought in from grass and given a thorough checking over. He is gradually acclimatized to the stable environment and is given low protein feed to begin with, which will be gradually increased as he gets fitter.

Start off his fitness programme by walking the roads. This is an ideal form of exercise for strengthening the muscles and tendons without causing strain. The walk should be brisk and rhythmical, starting with about three-quarters of an hour and building up to two hours. Continue walking for approximately two weeks, though for those whose ultimate aim is fast, hard work, this can be longer. Allow the horse one day off a week.

By weeks 3–4, he should be ready to start trotting. Warm him up in walk for at least half-an-hour, then proceed to trot for short periods, walking for longer periods in between. Gradually build up the trotting as fitness increases. Don't trot on roads for prolonged periods, however, as this could damage the horse's leg tendons and the delicate bones and structures of the feet. Trot up hills when on roads, if you have to, as this takes the pressure off the front legs. Sit two beats to change your diagonal regularly so that he doesn't become one-sided. By the fourth week you can also introduce some gentle work in the school, with a small amount of canter – don't exceed 20 minutes for the total session and go for a walking hack afterwards. By week five, start trotting up steep hills: this is an excellent way of building up the hindquarters. Carry on hacking and working in the school.

By week six the horse should be fit enough to cope with a canter work-out. This should be at a steady, controlled pace, but allow the horse to stretch out. Don't let cantering develop into a mad gallop. Walk him afterwards.

By now you should be confident that your horse is fit enough to begin some serious work. Commence with a proper schooling session lasting about 20 minutes and gradually build up to an hour. Concentrate on suppling movements with plenty of circles and turns, including serpentines. Ride in walk, trot, and canter. Once the horse is sufficiently toned up, introduce some gymnastic jumping exercises over grids, etc. This will greatly improve his balance and general athleticism.

The next and final stage should be tailor-made for the sport in which you planning to partake. Those interested in show-jumping should continue with athletic jumping exercises and schooling on the flat. This will build up the horse's muscles for jumping courses and also increase his balance. This is also beneficial for those who wish to event. However, this should be interspersed with periods of cantering, preferably on man-made gallops or soft ground – never canter on hard ground. Only gallop for a short while as this puts a tremendous amount of pressure on the horse's legs so that even a super-fit horse may become lame.

Once the horse has acquired his peak of fitness he should be allowed a little relaxation. Take him for some hacks or turn him out for a while, being careful not to press him too hard when he could easily loose confidence or become stale. Give him a rest day, but remember at the same time to reduce his feed.

Schooling on the flat and over trotting poles and small jumps will make a horse supple and responsive to its rider as well as adding interest to the fitness programme.

GROOMING

Your horse should be groomed at least once a day. This is not merely for cosmetic reasons but is an important part of his general care. The use of tack and rugs, causing a build-up of dirt and dust, could well cause irritation, resulting in painful swellings or galls. This is also an excellent opportunity to check for injuries, as well as being a good form of massage, stimulating the circulation and toning the muscles.

There are two methods of grooming the stabled horse. **Quartering** is a quick grooming before exercise to ensure that skin will be comfortable under tack and to give the horse a tidy appearance. First pick out the feet, then wash the face and under the dock, brushing the mane and tail. Undo rugs but don't take them off if the weather is at all cold; fold them back to expose the part you wish to groom, removing any stable

Whether or not you are exercising your horse, you should always groom him once a day, not only to ensure that he is clean and comfortable, but to check for injuries or signs that something may be otherwise amiss.

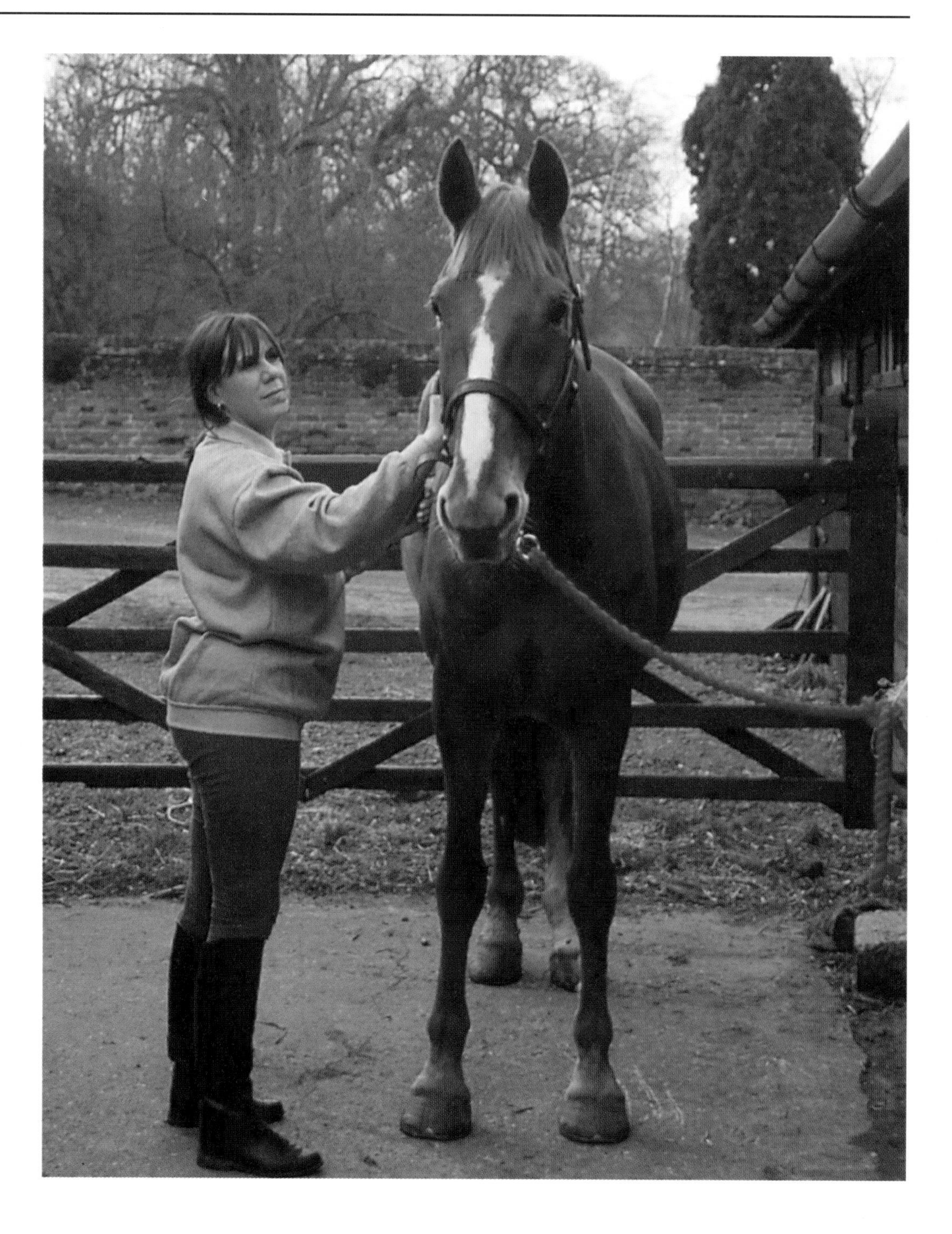

Quartering is a way of grooming a horse in winter without letting it get too cold. Remove the stable rug in sections, exposing only the parts you wish to groom, then replacing the rug as you go.

A few examples of grooming equipment: (top) hoof pick; (centre) hoof oil and brush; (below) dandy brush and rubber curry comb.

stains as you go before replacing them.

The other type of grooming, **strapping**, is done after exercise when dirt has become loosened from the coat. Give the horse a thorough brushing, starting with the hard dandy brush and removing all mud and dried-on sweat. Next use the soft body brush, working with short strokes along the lie of the coat. Work your way all over the horse, removing all excess dust and dirt. Clean the brush every other stroke with the metal curry comb. This process acts as a massage and also stimulates production of natural oils which help keep the coat healthy and shining. Take extra care with sensitive areas, such as the belly and back legs, as the horse may well be tempted to kick out. To groom the face, remove the headcollar so that it is buckled around the neck instead. Use the body brush, taking care around the sensitive eyes and ears. Clean the eyes and muzzle, nostrils and lips with a damp sponge. Next, sponge under and below the dock.

Finish with the mane and tail, removing all knots with your fingers, then brush thoroughly with the body brush, parting all the hairs and brushing out any excess knots and scurf.

Finally, run the horse over with a damp stable rubber to remove any remaining dust and to give an extra shine. Pick out and oil the hooves: some claim that it is inadvisable to do this too often as the oil forms a barrier, preventing the hoof from losing natural moisture. Check with your farrier that your horse's feet are able to withstand constant oiling. If you are still uncertain, use oil only for special occasions, such as shows. When oiling, make sure that the hooves are thoroughly clean, as well as dry, making sure that they are evenly coated from heel to coronet. You can also oil the soles of the foot which helps stop mud and straw adhering. Remember that horses are unpredictable and can often be irritable when groomed. Take special care that you don't get kicked or bitten.

The grooming kit

A good set of grooming tools is vital. Check that your brushes are not worn

GROOMING

▼ The sequence below provides step-by-step instructions on how to groom a muddy horse which has been brought in from the field. Nowadays, most people turn their horses out during the day and bring them in at night; this is termed the combined method. The kind of grooming illustrated is therefore the one you are most likely to use.

and that they are cleaned regularly. Use each piece of equipment for the purpose for which it is intended. Using an incorrect brush at the wrong stage of the grooming process will not only be ineffectual but could also harm the horse's sensitive skin.

Keep your kit all together in a handy container, marking each piece with the horse's name. Never use his grooming kit on any other horse This could spread skin diseases, as well as lice infestation.

Hoof pick Usually made of metal, with a plastic-covered handle, make sure that the end is blunt as a sharp instrument could easily cut the frog and sole of the hoof. (*See p. 73.*)

Curry comb This is manufactured from plastic or rubber. After picking out the horse's feet, this is the first piece of grooming equipment you would choose. Use it to remove thick mud and loose hair from the coat of a horse which has been turned out. Take care around sensitive areas as it is a harsh tool, and never use it on fine coats or on horses which have been clipped.

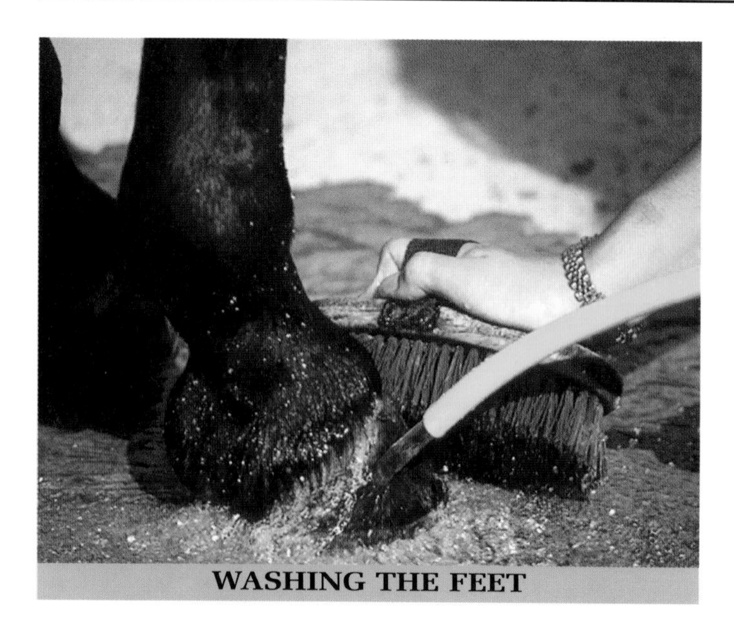

WASHING THE FEET

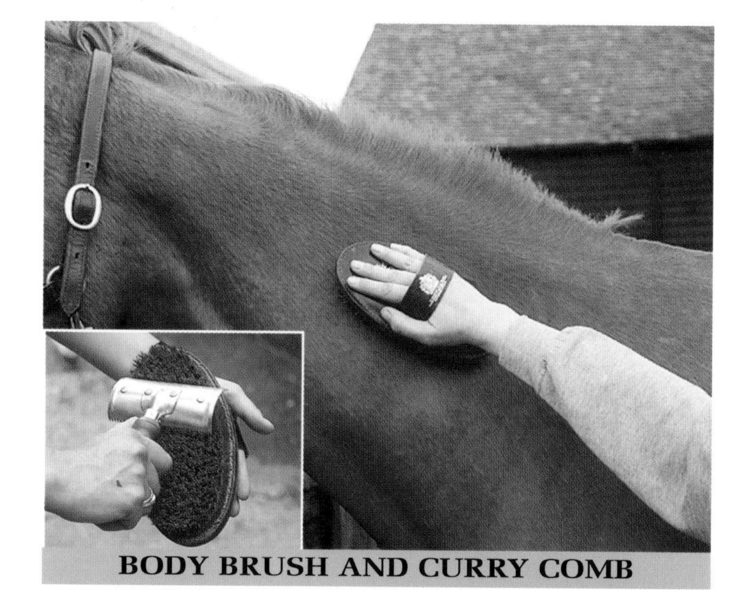

BODY BRUSH AND CURRY COMB

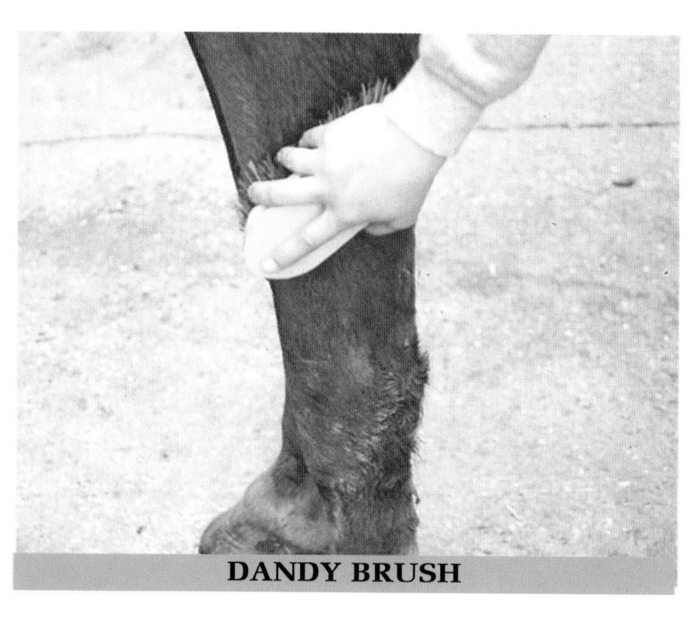

DANDY BRUSH

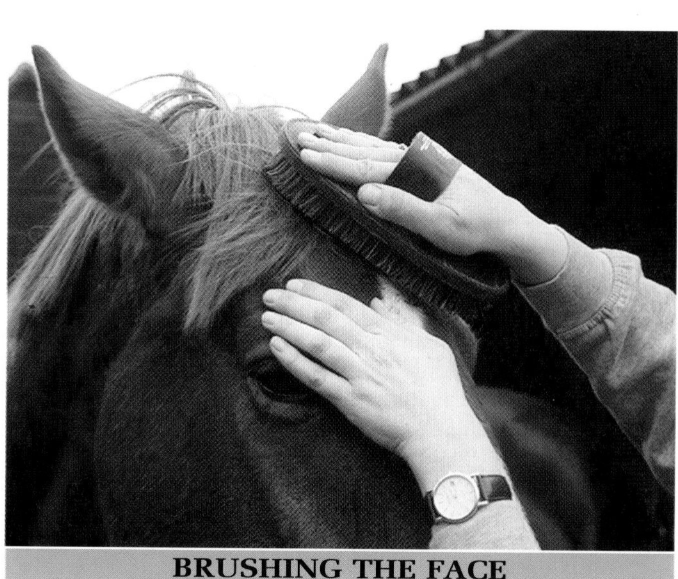

BRUSHING THE FACE

Dandy brush This is a long, coarse-bristled brush, made from either natural or synthetic materials. It is also used for removing any excess mud that was left behind by the rubber curry comb. It can be used on all kinds of coat, although care must be taken on sensitive areas, especially if the horse is clipped. Most horses quite enjoy the scratchy feel of the dandy brush.

Body brush This has short, dense and soft bristles. Used in conjunction with a metal curry comb, it removes all the dust, dirt and scurf from the horse's coat. It also helps to release the skin's natural oils, making the coat healthy and lustrous. It is worth investing in a good quality body brush with natural bristles which will do the job more effectively.

Metal curry comb This is solely for cleaning out the body brush – never use it on the horse. Clean the body brush after every two or three strokes, drawing the metal curry comb through the bristles away from your body as the metal teeth of the curry are very sharp and could easily cut your wrist. To

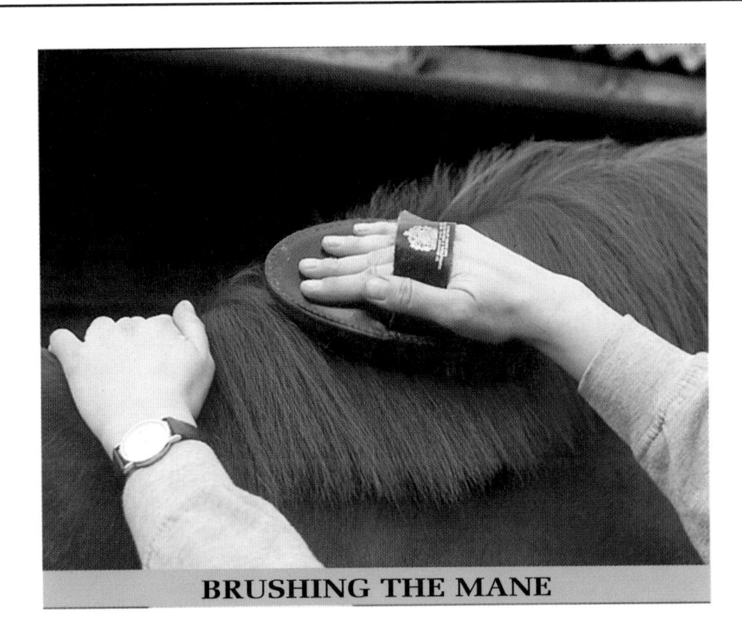

BRUSHING THE MANE

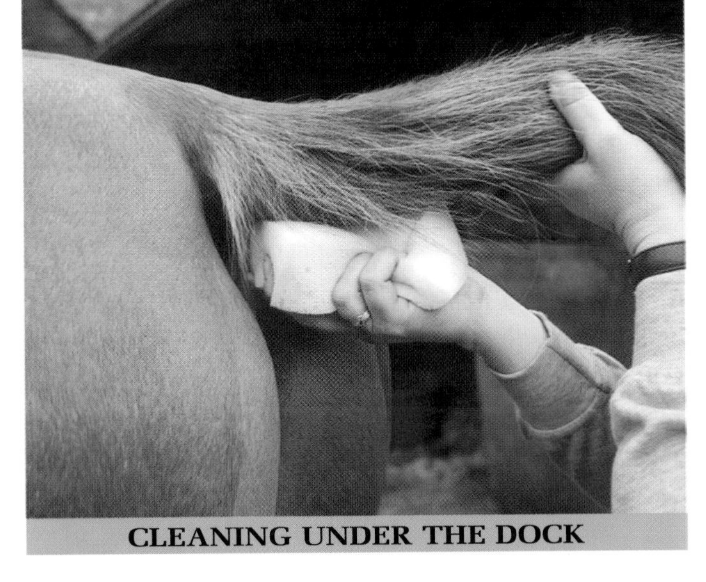

CLEANING UNDER THE DOCK

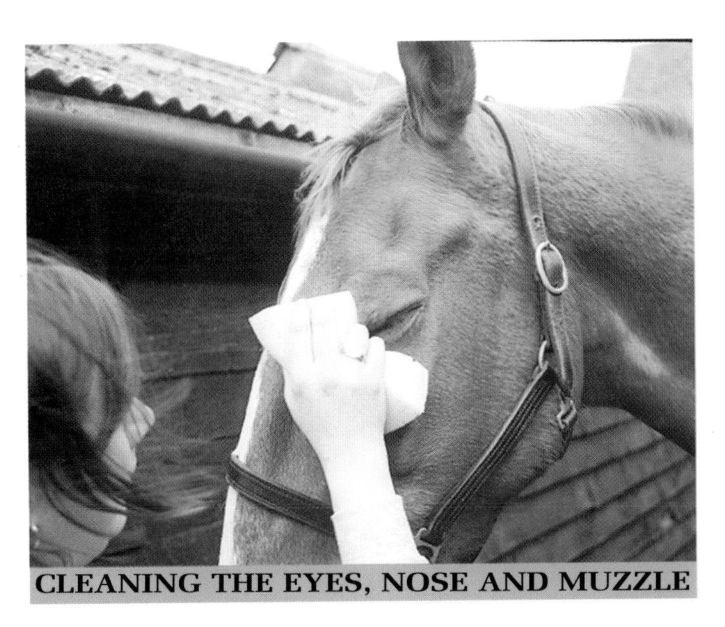

CLEANING THE EYES, NOSE AND MUZZLE

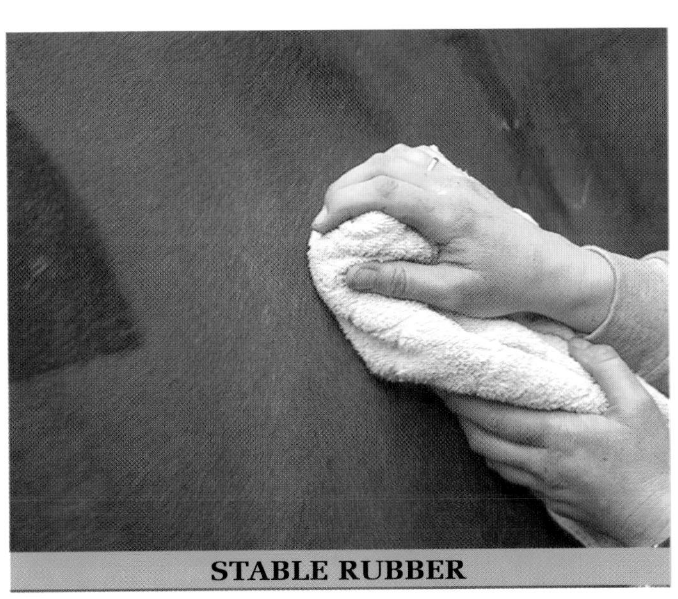

STABLE RUBBER

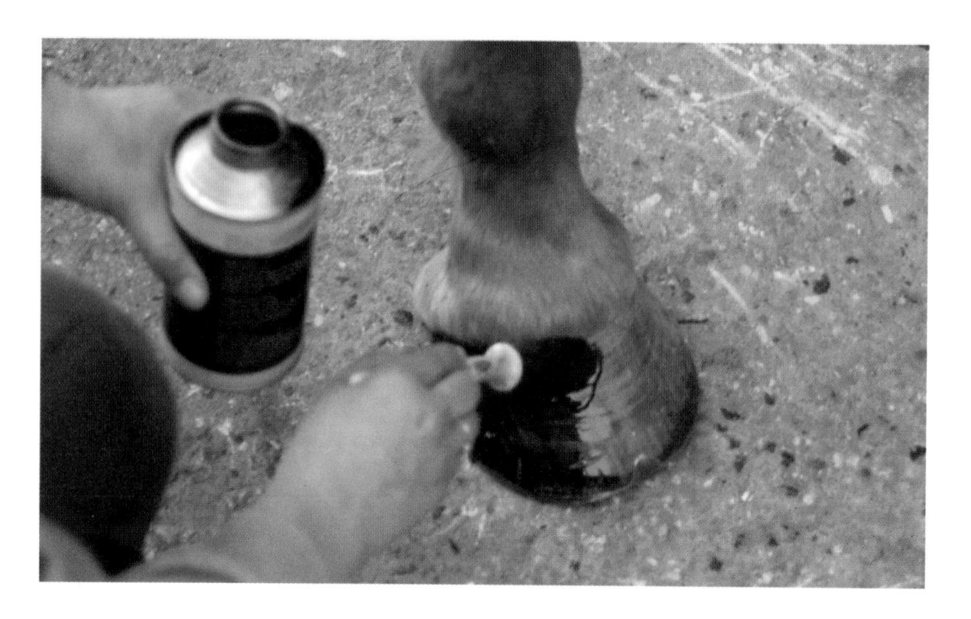

▲ There are varying opinions as to the wisdom of oiling feet. While it certainly is of little benefit to the horse itself, some claim it may be harmful if practised on a regular basis. The best advice is to oil feet only for shows, or on the odd occasion when you wish your horse to look particularly smart.

remove the excess dirt from the curry, knock its end on any hard surface or on the ground.

Water brush This brush can be used for a number of purposes and usually has plastic bristles. It is used damp to lay the mane and tail, or to remove stable stains from the coat. It can also be used with a bucket of water or a hose to clean muddy hooves.

Sponges You will require two of these, one for cleaning the eyes, nose and mouth, and one for the dock area. It is a good idea to buy them in different colours so that you don't get them mixed up. Make sure that each sponge is thoroughly cleaned after use and that they are not stored next to one another.

Stable rubber This is a cloth, usually of cotton or linen – an old dish towel will do. Used slightly damp, it is rubbed over the coat to pick up any residual dust and to give a final shine.

Hoof oil This is for cosmetic purposes, used to make hooves shine. It does nothing to improve the horn of the hoof. The oil is available in clear, brown or black and of a liquid or thick consistency. Apply with a brush.

Massage pad Made from leather, it has mostly replaced the traditional hay wisp. It is used to tone the muscles and improve the circulation of a horse which is in work.

Wisping

A wisp can be made from hay which is knotted to make a pad, or a leather pad with an easy-to-hold handle is available from most saddlers. This a good method of toning the muscles and should only be used on the quarters, thighs, neck and shoulders. First bang the wisp quite hard down onto the coat, following with a short stroke along the lie of the coat. Starting with about five bangs per area, you can increase their frequency as the horse becomes more accustomed to them.

TIP

A dirty knotted tail can be easily disentangled by applying a little baby oil from a spray bottle. Massage it into the hair with your hand and brush it through. The knots will fall out easily, leaving a tangle-free shiny result. There are other products on the market designed for the purpose; however, baby oil is much the cheaper option.

Pulling the mane

Horses with thick manes often look untidy – the mane won't lie flat and it is difficult to plait. Pulling the mane will not only thin it out, but also shorten it, leaving it more manageable and looking smarter. To pull the mane, take a few hairs at a time from underneath, winding them around a comb and pulling sharply. Work down the mane, repeating the process. If the horse has a particularly thick mane, it is a good idea to pull it gradually over a few days; this will prevent him getting impatient or distressed.

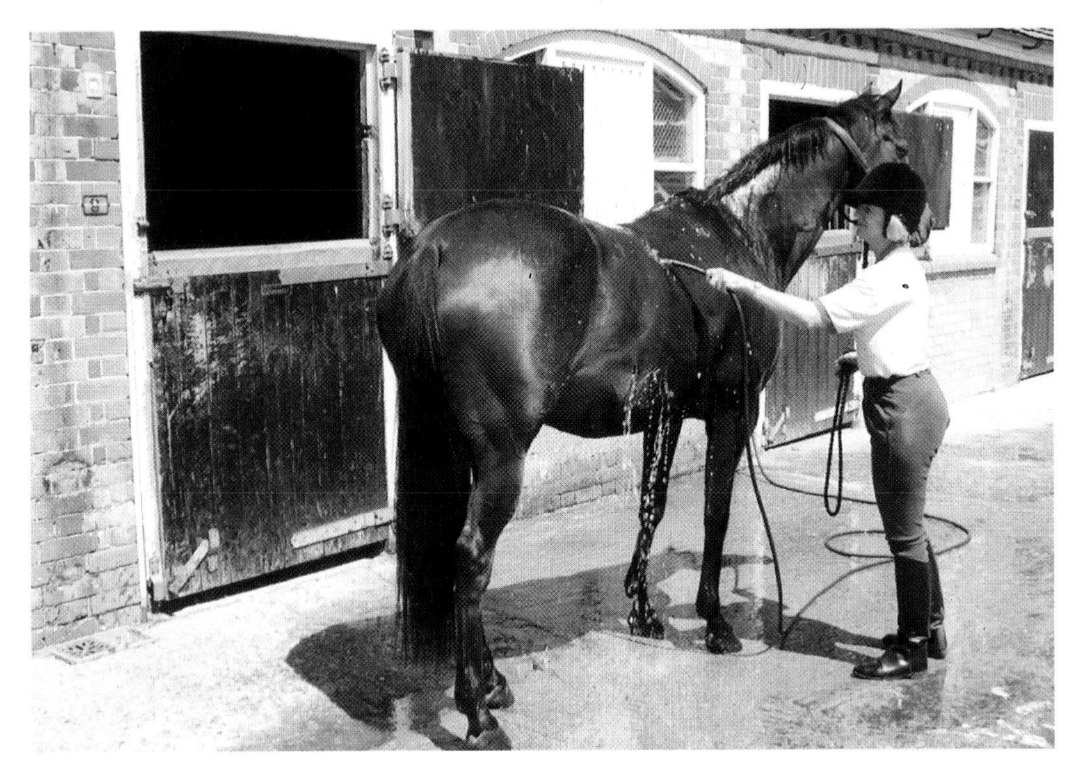

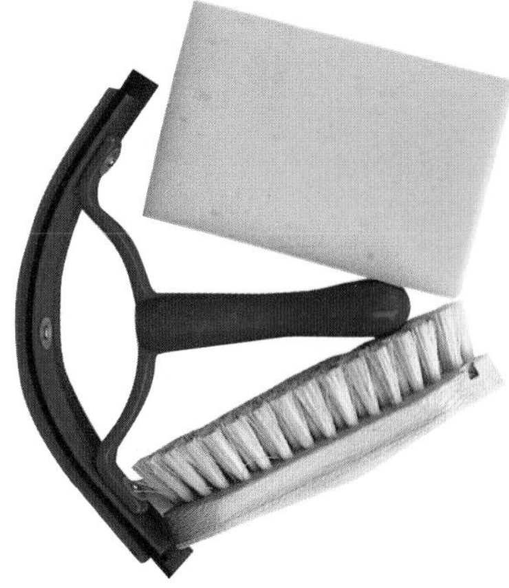

Your horse will enjoy a bath, providing it is a warm sunny day. Use a mild shampoo especially for the purpose and make sure that it is rinsed away before using the sweat scraper. Pictured above is a sponge, water brush and sweat scraper for removing excess water.

Pulling the tail
This can be painful and should be done over several days, pulling only a few hairs at a time. Take the hairs from underneath only. A kinder option is to plait the tail for shows.

Bathing your horse
On a hot day, your horse will enjoy a bath. There are many mild horse shampoos available containing insecticides and fly repellents. Wet the horse thoroughly, using a bucket of water and a sponge. Some horses don't mind at all being hosed, but try to maintain a gentle flow of water so as not to alarm him. Apply a little shampoo and lather it into the coat, mane and tail, using a sponge. Take care with the area around the eyes and ears. Rinse off thoroughly then, using a sweat scraper, remove all excess water. If the weather is hot, allow to dry naturally; if cool, use an anti-sweat rug to prevent the horse from becoming chilled.

Finally, once he is dry, brush him over with a *clean* body brush and brush out the mane and tail. Don't bathe your horse too often as this will deplete the natural oils in his coat. A thorough grooming will give almost as good as result. Don't attempt to bathe your horse in anything but the warmest of weather.

HOW TO PICK OUT A HORSE'S FEET

Front feet Stand with your back to the horse's head, reaching around the back of the leg and sliding your hand down the inside to the pastern while applying firm pressure to encourage the horse to lift his foot. Support the hoof with your hand, with your palm on the inside. Using a hoof pick, remove dirt first from around the frog, using a downward action towards the toe.

Back feet Stand close to the horse's side and slide your near hand down the quarters, eventually running down the inside leg. Once it reaches the fetlock, apply pressure to encourage him to raise his foot. Support the foot and pick out in the same manner as the front.

CLIPPING

▼ Horse clippers and replacement blades are extremely expensive, though a good quality pair will last for many years and save money in the long run. Clippers should be serviced regularly and should be cleaned thoroughly after each use. They should be lubricated regularly, using a good quality clipper oil.

If your horse is in work and is stabled in winter, you will soon realize that he cannot go even for a light hack without sweating profusely, particularly if he is of a non-Thoroughbred breed. A horse which is constantly sweated-up will rapidly lose condition and, being permanently damp, is more likely to catch a chill. It is for this reason that clipping is so important.

There are several types of clip, each geared to the amount of work the horse does, from a small 'trace' clip (where the areas most prone to sweating are removed) to the full clip where almost all the hair is removed.

Before clipping, choose your location carefully. Check that there is a power source nearby and that it is fitted with a circuit-breaker. Remove all hazards such as water buckets, wheel-barrows, etc. The best location is a well-lit stable. When clipping, always wear a hard hat and it is a good idea to wear a pair of overalls as well as rubber boots. When holding the clippers, always thread the loop handle through your hand. (If the horse were suddenly to jump you could easily drop a very expensive piece of equipment.)

Before clipping, try to discover what the horse's reaction is likely to be. If he is likely to be difficult he may have to be restrained or even sedated by your vet. If the horse has never been clipped before, get him used to the sound by switching on the clippers, but without letting them touch him. Once he has become accustomed to this, lay the clippers against his side when they are

HOW TO CLIP YOUR HORSE

1 Prepare the horse, making sure that he is well groomed, with all mud, sweat and dust removed from the coat. Bandage the tail to keep it out of the way. Ask an assistant to hold him. Decide which clip is most suitable and mark the outline with chalk, making sure that it is symmetrical.

2 Start to clip, beginning at the shoulder and clipping against the lie of the hair with the blades parallel to the horse's body and taking care not to catch the skin. Get the feel of the clippers on an unnoticeable area before clipping up to the chalk mark.

3 Take care with delicate areas such as under the jowl and between the legs. Use your other hand to stretch the skin and get an assistant to hold up the front legs while you do under the 'armpits'.

4 When clipping the face, decide if you want to do a full-face clip, only under the chin, or a half-face clip. Attempt a full-face clip only with the most well behaved of horses. For a half-face, you will need to put on the bridle. Clip up to the cheek-pieces. For the face it is best to use a smaller pair of clippers.

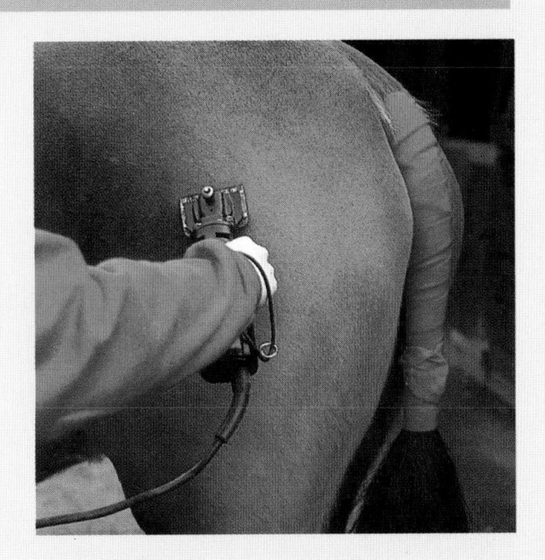

◄ Before starting to clip, make sure that the horse is thoroughly clean and that its tail is bandaged. You should be wearing overalls, a hard hat and stout rubber boots to protect youself from accidental electric shock. Loop the handle of the clippers through your wrist so that you don't drop them.

◄ Never clip alone. Ask an assistant to hold the horse and to soothe him should he becomes upset. If the horse is prone to misbehaviour, hold him in a bridle.

turned off to give him an idea of their sensation. Luckily, a horse that has once been clipped is unlikely to be a problem in future.

Trace clip
This is the lightest clip. Horses sweat mostly under the neck, belly and thighs, so these are the only areas where the hair is removed. For an even lighter clip you could remove only the undersides of the neck and chest. This is ideal for horses and ponies in light work, or which are turned out for much of the day. A clipped horse must be rugged up and should always be kept in at night, and covered with a New Zealand rug when turned out during the day.

Blanket clip
This clip is shaped literally as though a blanket had been thrown over the

▼ The trace clip is ideal for horses engaged in light work in winter. Only the hair on thighs, belly and under the neck is removed, leaving behind as much of the horse's natural protection as possible.

horse's back. The horse has half his face, all his neck, shoulders, belly and thighs clipped. This clip allows the horse to work hard without sweating, but keeps his loins and quarters warm when being walked for long periods. Because he has had quite a lot of hair removed, he should be kept warm with a good quality night rug and turned out in a thick New Zealand.

Hunter clip

The horse is completely clipped out, leaving only the saddle area and legs for protection. Special care must be taken to ensure that he is warm enough. He should be rugged up at all times and, if exercised at walk, should wear an exercise sheet to keep his loins and quarters warm.

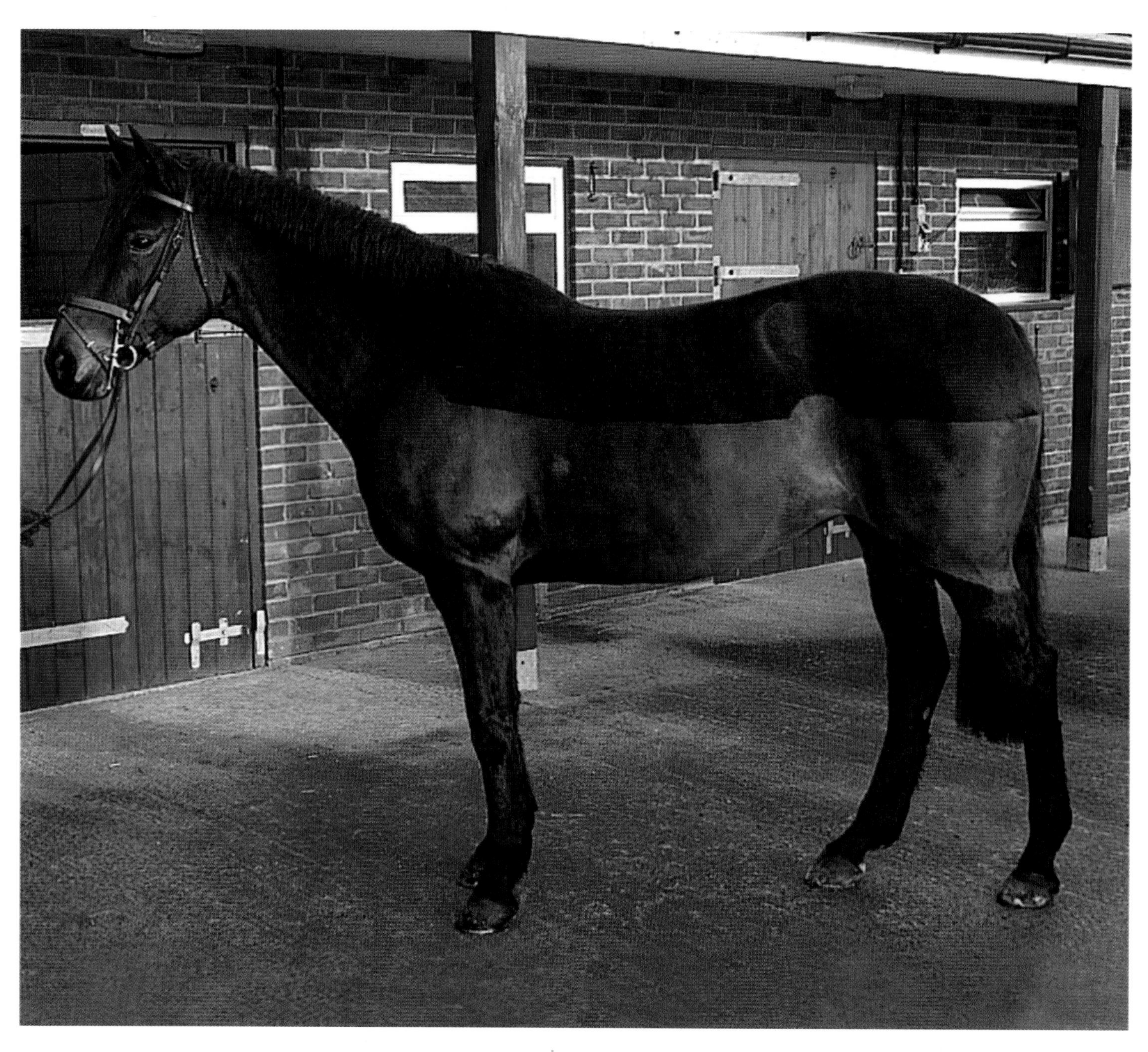

The blanket clip is probably the most popular and versatile. Half the face, the neck, belly and part of the back legs are clipped, but the loins remain unclipped and act like a blanket to keep the horse warm. This is the ideal clip for horses in medium work.

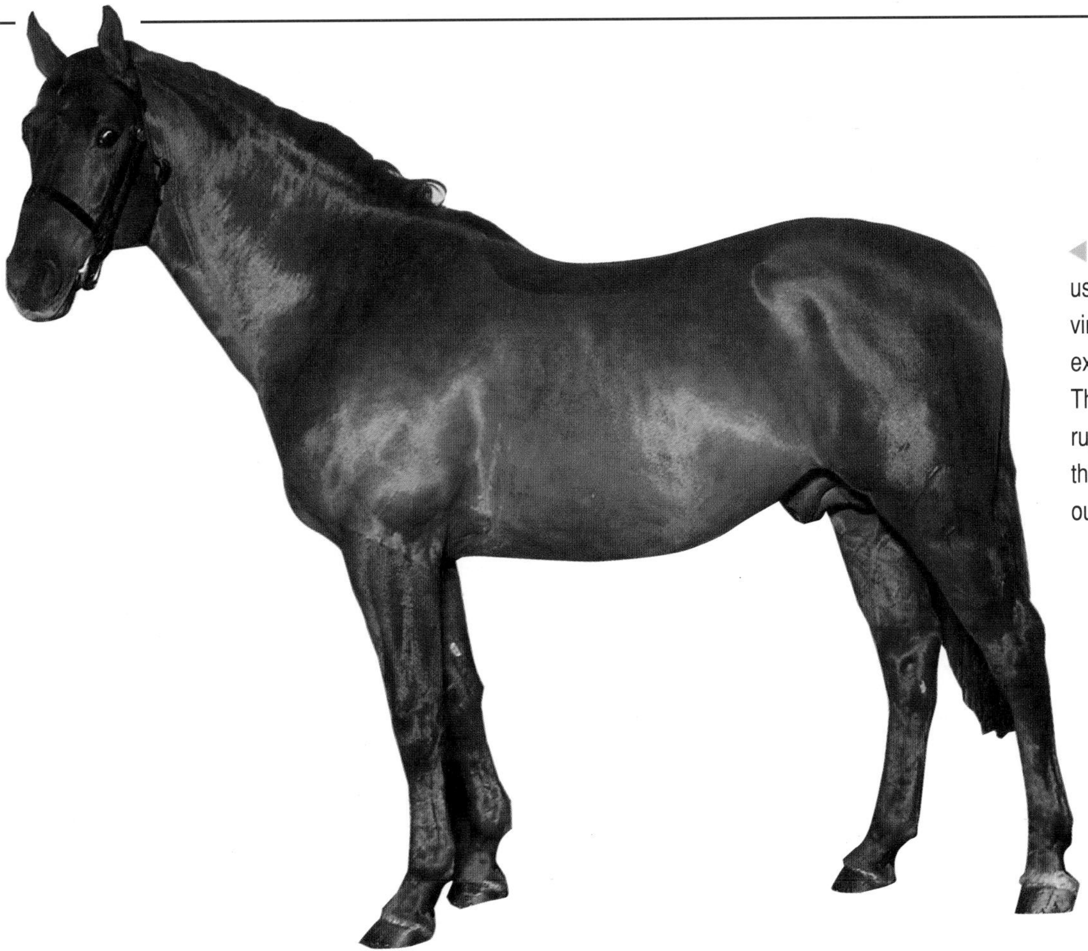

The hunter clip should only be used for horses in hard work, when virtually all the hair is removed except for the saddle and leg areas. The horse should be thoroughly rugged, and it is not recommended that a horse with this clip is turned out.

RUGS AND BLANKETS

▼ The New Zealand rug is vital to all horses turned out during winter. Even thick-coated animals will require one in extreme weather conditions. Thanks to new lightweight fibres, the New Zealand is no longer the heavy sodden tarpaulin it used to be. Many rugs came with hood attachments (inset left) to give extra protection. Fasten leg straps (inset right) by passing one around each back leg, making sure they are looped together.

There are many different types of rugs available and your choice will depend upon your horse's circumstances – whether stabled, at grass, or clipped – and his breed will also have a bearing on the one you choose.

New Zealand rug This is traditionally made of green canvas. Nowadays, however, a variety of man-made materials are also used, and they are just as hard-wearing and waterproof. Ideally, New Zealands are lined with wool for extra warmth but, again, synthetic fabrics are just as often used. This type of rug is for horses who are out at grass in the winter when it will protect them from harsh weather, particularly rain. A horse in a New Zealand rug should be checked at least twice a day to ensure that the rug has not slipped. The best New Zealands have cross-over leg straps which loop between the horse's back legs. Other means of securing the rugs are cross-over straps passing under the horse's belly, or a built-in surcingle can also be used.

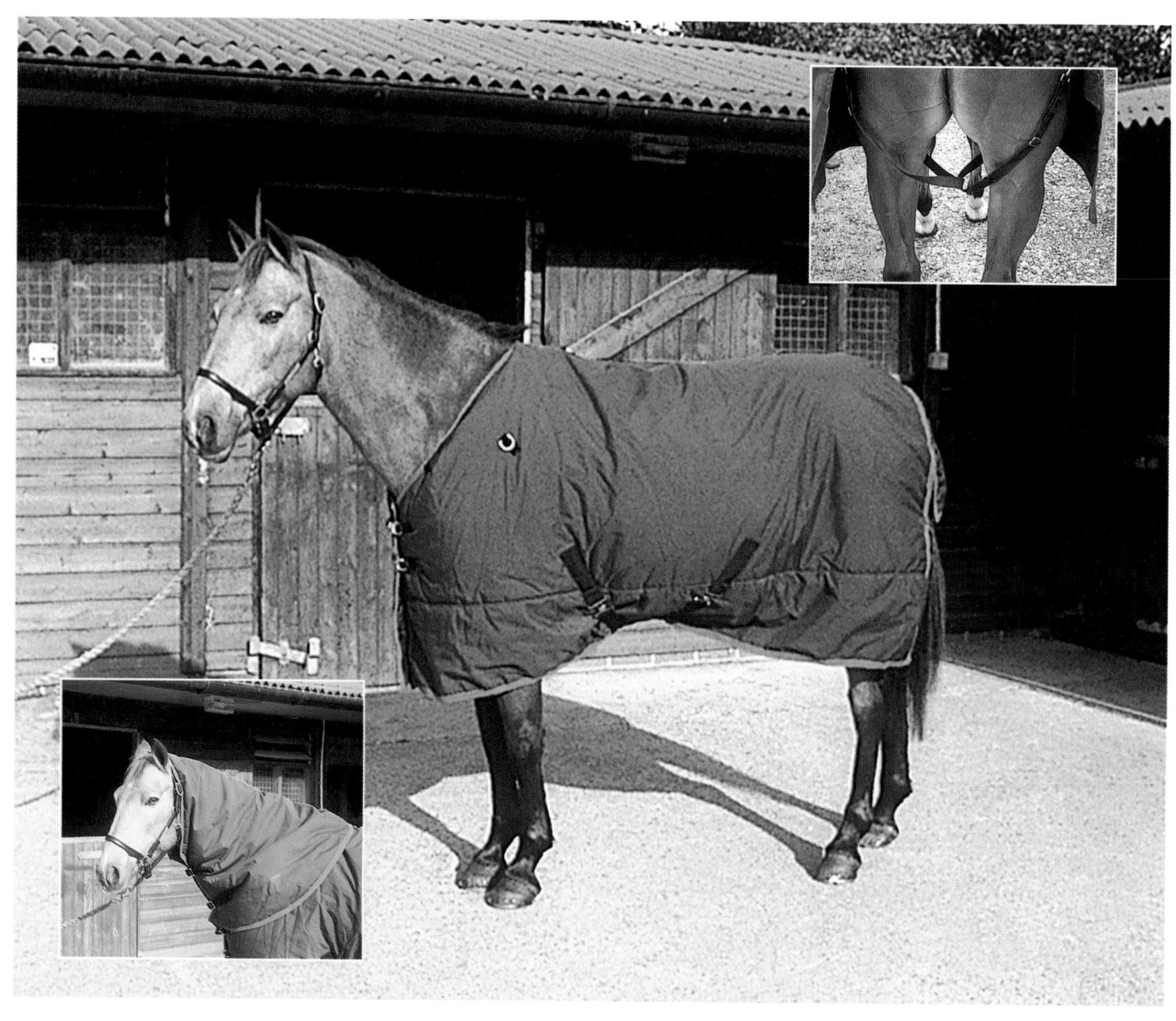

◀ The modern lightweight stable rug is warm and easy to maintain. This one has a hood attachment which is ideal for horses whose necks have been clipped and will add extra warmth on especially cold days.

▼ A wool stable rug. These are extremely warm and useful as travelling rugs.

Stable rug This is designed for horses which are kept in and the nylon quilted version with a cotton lining is the most popular. These rugs are relatively cheap to buy, are lightweight, and are easily washed. More than one can be worn in very cold weather. The traditional pure wool stable rug provides a great deal of warmth and also allows the skin to breathe. They are so smart that they can be used at competition venues to keep a horse warm while he is standing around waiting to compete. Its disadvantage is that it is rather difficult to wash and is liable to shrink if washed in water which is too hot. Moreover, the horse's bedding can easily become entangled in the weave. The jute rug is the cheapest type of stable rug available. It is very warm, though heavy and difficult to wash. This kind of rug is usually secured with a roller. Make sure a protective pad is put under the roller to protect the spine.

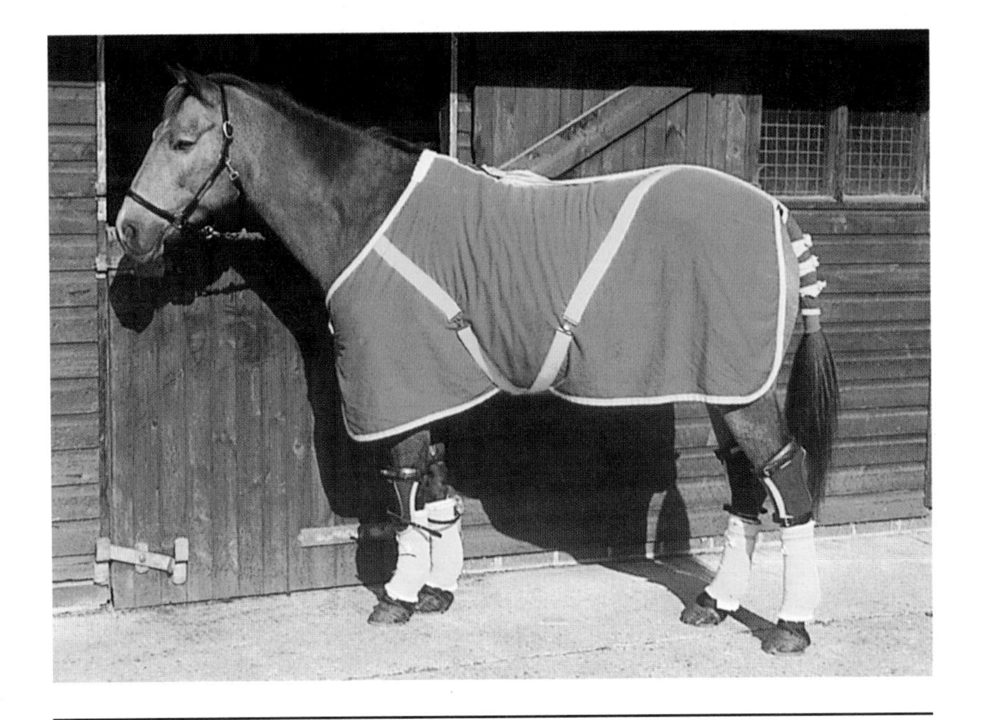

Summer Sheet The summer sheet is manufactured from light cotton, usually with cross-over straps and a fillet string. It comes in a variety of colours and is easy to maintain.

▶ The summer sheet will keep your horse's coat clean, helping it to maintain its gloss before a show. It can be used in summer to protect horses from flies.

▼ The sweat sheet allows a horse to cool down and dry off without catching a chill and should be used under another rug. If you are leaving your horse unattended, apply a roller to prevent the rug slipping off.

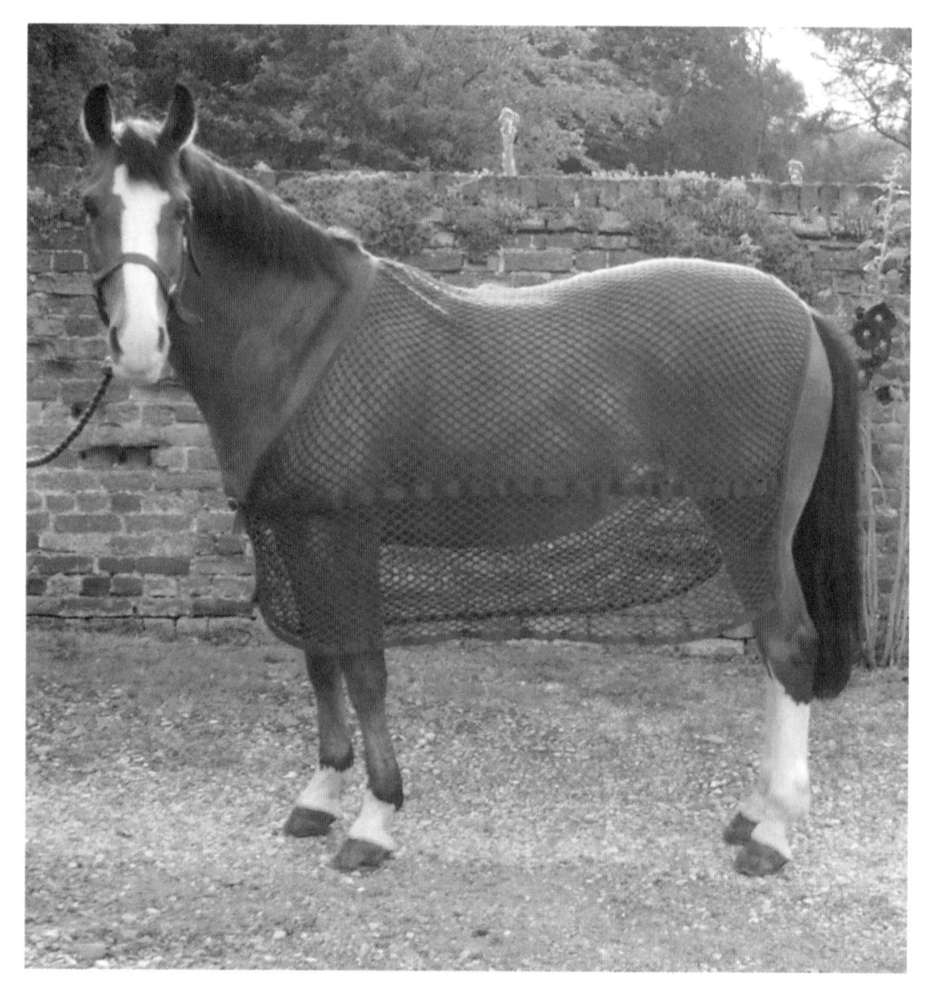

The sheet is useful in hot weather for protecting horses from flies when they are out in the field. It can also be used to keep dust out of horses' coats when travelling. Show competitors sometimes use the summer sheet to throw over their ponies to keep them clean and tidy while awaiting their turn.

Sweat sheet The sweat sheet is a loosely woven cotton rug, rather like a string vest, and comes in many different colours. It is used when horses have been sweating profusely and need to cool off slowly. It should be used with another rug on top. Air is trapped in the pockets of the weave which helps the animal to dry off, preventing him from cooling down too rapidly and becoming chilled.

◀ Despite the snow, this horse is snug and warm in his New Zealand rug. New technology has produced rugs which are lightweight, robust and warm.

SADDLERY

Saddlery is often referred to as 'tack', and covers a range of equipment likely to prove daunting to the novice. New technology has allowed a wide range of new materials and gadgets which, in the main, have made life easier for the equestrian. Brushing-boots, girths, saddles and many other pieces of equipment are now commonly made of man-made fibres instead of leather, which has made cleaning and maintenance a good deal easier. However, those of us who prefer traditional saddlery made from leather and other natural fibres will still find them available.

Saddlery must be fitted well to horse and rider. It is no use having a saddle that is perfect for the horse but too small for the rider and vice versa. If you are interested in a wide range of activities, it is best to choose a general-purpose saddle. However, if you decide to specialize in dressage or jumping you may decide to invest in a saddle for that specific purpose. The dressage saddle is straight-cut and allows the rider's leg to fall straighter and longer. In contrast,

▶ Pictured here is the most commonly used bridle, fitted with a flash noseband and an eggbut snaffle bit.

Points of the bridle

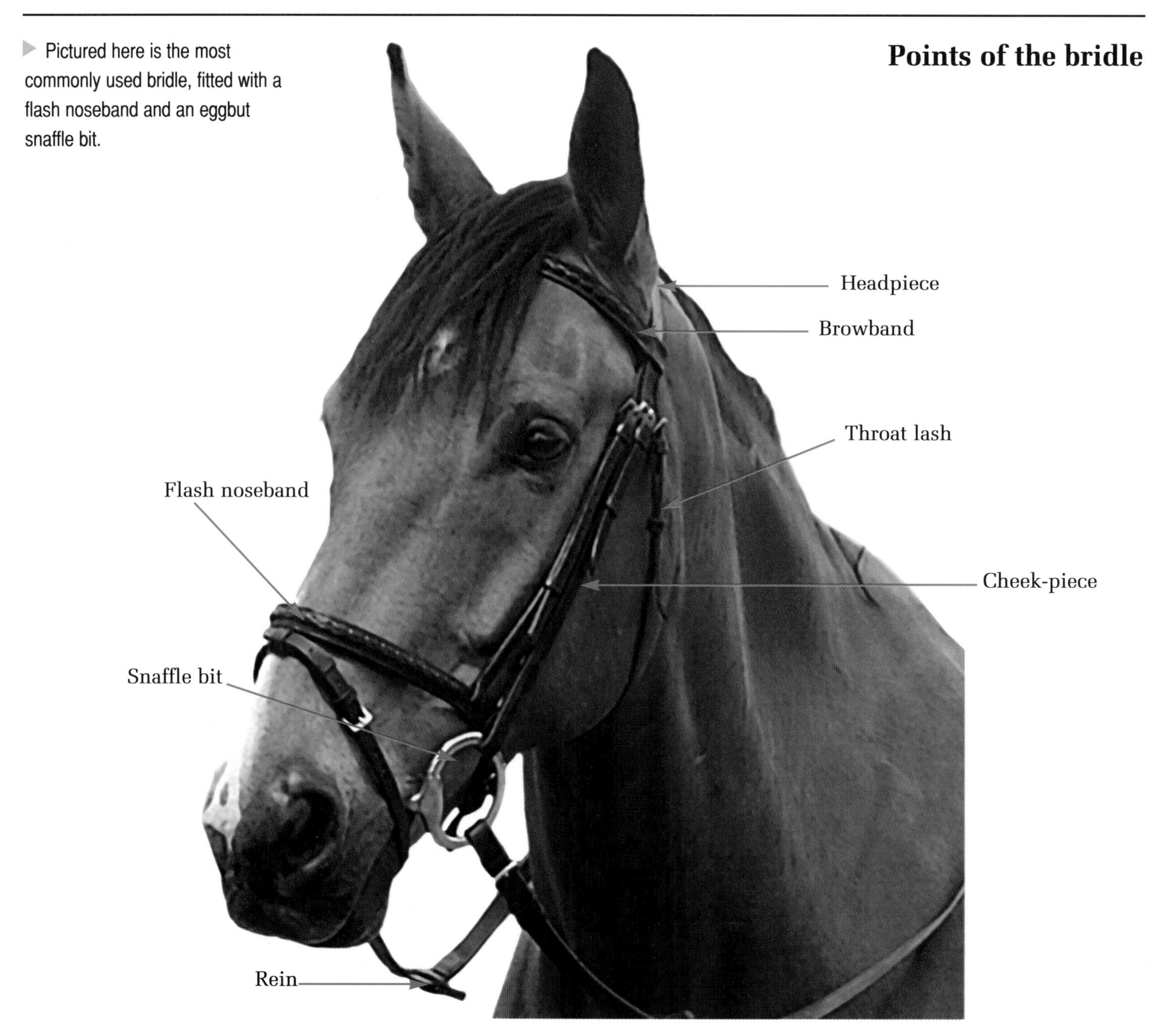

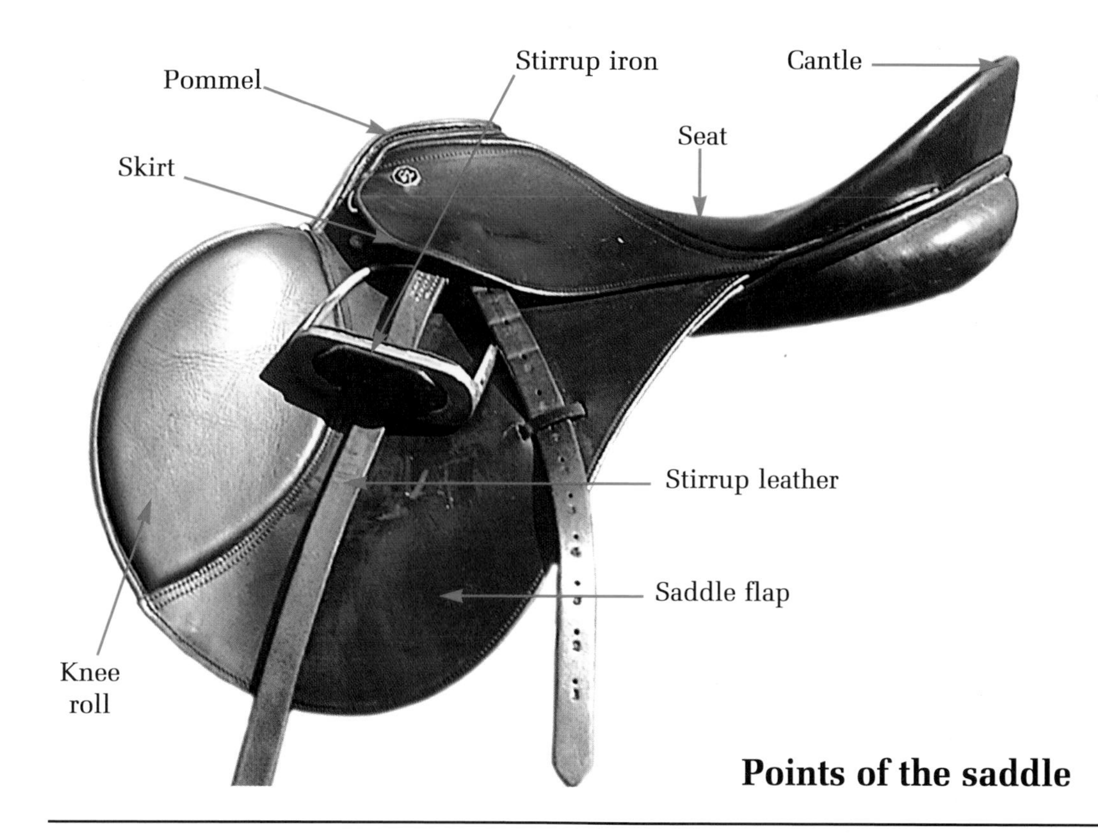

◀ This jumping saddle is the most forward cut of the saddles and helps keep the rider in balance when jumping.

Points of the saddle

the jumping saddle encourages a shorter stirrup length for better balance while jumping.

Western Saddlery is becoming ever more popular in Europe and has much decorative appeal.

Western bridles usually have a snaffle or curb bit with long curved cheek-pieces. There are two types of Western bridle – the California-style which has a single length of rein known as a 'romal' and the Texas-style which has split reins.

There are many different designs of Western saddle, but the basic difference is the high horn, high cantle, and a deep wide seat. They are intended for long hours out on the range and are therefore well padded for comfort and heavier than European saddles.

Saddlery is liable to deterioration over a period of time and it is therefore essential to keep it in the best possible condition at all times. Regular cleaning, saddle-soaping and coating with leather dressing will help maintain

◀ For those who like to do a bit of everything, the general-purpose saddle can be used for most disciplines.

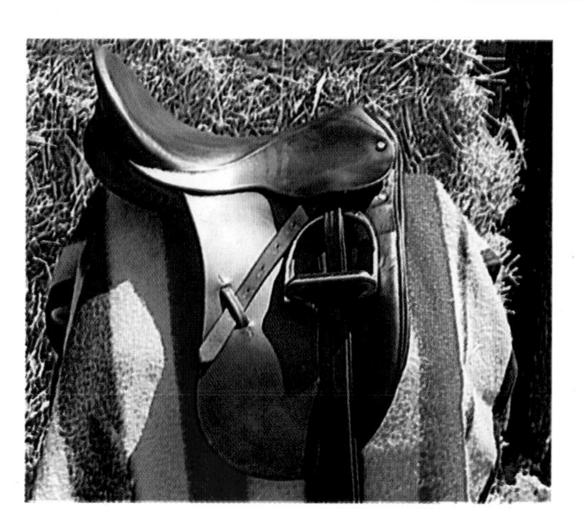

◀ The dressage saddle is for flat work only. It is straight-cut to allow for a longer leg and stirrup, an upright position and deep seat.

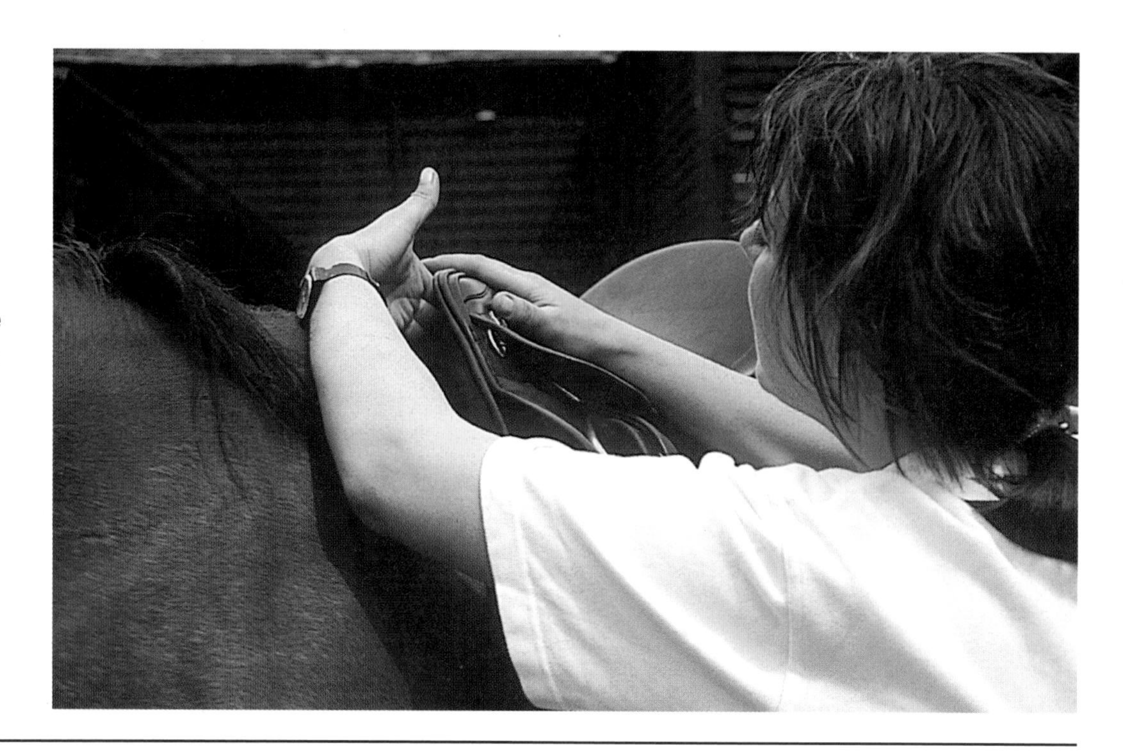

▶ Fitting a saddle is not to be undertaken lightly: a poorly-fitting saddle can not only do long-term damage to your horse, but will also effect the position of the rider. A good saddler will have been trained to fit a saddle correctly.

The saddle should not touch the horse's spine, and the gusset should fit correctly all the way along the back. The weight-bearing surface should distribute the rider's weight and match the contours of horse's back. It should fit snugly without rocking, and with no side-to-side movement.

▲ Cleaning your tack should be done regularly, not only to preserve its life but also for the horse's comfort. It is also a good opportunity to check for wear or damaged stitching.

suppleness and prolong its life. Stitching must be regularly checked to ensure safety. A poorly stitched stirrup leather or bridle could have disastrous consequences should splitting or breakage occur while it is in use. Well maintained tack, however old, always looks smart and will invariably hold a good second-hand value.

Fitting a saddle must be done by an expert who is either a master saddler or otherwise qualifed. The saddle should first be inspected for soundness and that it is symmetrical when looking along the gullet or channel. Check that the stuffing is even on both sides and, if it is second-hand, make sure all stitching is in good condition. There are various tests to prove that the tree is sound, but these are best left to an expert.

Care of Tack

All leatherwork should be examined carefully after use and it is recommended that you clean your tack each time you ride.

Cleaning the bridle When cleaning a bridle, carefully check all stitching and look out for brittle or damaged leather which could indicate a weak spot. Anything that needs attention should either be repaired by a reputable saddler or replaced.

Take the bridle completely apart. Put the bit into clean water to soak while you set about the bridle. Lay the individual pieces out in front of you. Thoroughly clean all the dirt and old saddle soap away from each piece.

When the entire bridle is really clean, apply new saddle soap and gently polish it to a glossy finish. Clean the bit with soapy water, and rinse and polish it with a clean cloth. Do not use metal polish on any parts which come into contact with the horse's mouth.

Cleaning the saddle

First take the girth, numnah, stirrups and leathers from the saddle, then wash the saddle and leathers lightly with a damp sponge to remove all mud and dirt. Rub saddle soap into the leather and polish well. Next, brush off the numnah and girth strap, removing all loose hair and dirt. If they are very dirty they can be washed in soapy water, rinsed, and hung out to dry. Remember to wash and dry the stirrup irons and give them a good polish. When all is clean, reassemble.

Girths

There are many kinds of girths from which to choose, designed for different types of horses and variously priced. They range from webbing girths to those made of leather. It is important that you choose the girth that is the most comfortable and safest you can find.

The double bridle

The double bridle

This form of bitting should not be used until the horse is working in a snaffle bridle. The rider must be adept at controlling two sets of reins independently of one another and with sensitivity.

It is mainly used in advanced dressage and in the show-ring, and will enhance the horse's performance. It should not be used to bully the horse. The bridoon bit acts as a snaffle, while the curb encourages flexion by a combination of the bars of the bit and the curb on the chin groove.

If your horse has never worn a curb before, it is a good idea to lead him in-hand first and then to ride in walk for a while until he gets used to it.

The bridoon should be fitted like a snaffle with the curb slightly lower, making sure that both bits are clear of the tushes (teeth). The curb chain should sit comfortably in the chin groove and under no circumstance be twisted.

◀ Girths are made from leather or synthetic materials. They should always be kept clean and checked regularly for wear. Threadbare girths should be discarded and damaged stitching repaired.

The short girth (far left) is for a dressage saddle which traditionally has a long girth strap.

Nosebands

Nosebands come in many styles and are designed to exert varying degrees of control. The usual kind of noseband is the cavesson. It fits around the nose above the bit.

A flash is a cavesson noseband fitted with a drop attachment and means that a standing martingale can be fitted to the cavesson section. This must not be fitted to low.

A drop noseband prevents the horse from opening his mouth. The front section must be fitted quite high to

▲ A useful way to exercise your horse, as well as being a base from which to school the young horse, is by lungeing him. This horse is wearing a correctly fitted lunge cavesson and a bridle. Note that the bridle should be put on over the cavesson.

prevent the noseband from interfering with the horse's breathing. The back strap should rest in the chin groove and not be too tight. It must be loose enough to allow the horse to relax his jaw but firm enough to prevent the horse from crossing his jaw or opening his mouth.

A grakle will prevent jaw-crossing and is more effective than the simple drop noseband.

Bits

When choosing a bit, it is important to go for the mildest one your horse will respect. It should sit comfortably in a wet mouth with the horse chomping calmly, a sign that he is happy with it. When you take up the reins, the horse should accept a contact calmly and with the jaws relaxed and slightly parted.

Snatching at the bit with clenched jaws indicates that it may be too severe or ill-fitting. Check that it isn't too wide: this could enable it to be pulled through, rubbing the mouth. A bit which is too tight will pinch.

Once established, don't change a bit for the sake of it. Most problems can be resolved by schooling and changing to a more severe bit is not always the answer.

It you are unsure of a bit's strength, start with the mildest first and proceed until you find one which is perfect.

Snaffles These range from very mild to very severe. They come jointed, straight or mullen-mouth. The mildest of these are most suitable for young horses, or horses being ridden by novice riders, as such a bit can do little damage to the horse if it were to panic or be pulled in the mouth. There are many which work on the corners of the mouth, squeezing it gently. More severe versions will also apply a little pressure to the tongue.

Pelham This acts in a way similar to the double bridle, but with only one bit it is not as effective. It is useful for less experienced riders and for horses unwilling to accept the double bridle. It is relatively mild and allows more control than the milder snaffles. A leather coupling can be attached so that only one rein can be used, though this seems to reduce the effect.

Gag This bit is for horses which pull hard and lower their heads. They are based on the snaffle and their severity will depend on the thickness of the bit. They work by applying continuous pressure on the poll and upward pressure on the mouth, making the horse raise his head.

Bitless bridle This is a good option for horses with extremely soft or damaged mouths. They can also have a dramatic effect on a horse which pulls. They apply a combination of pressure on the nose and chin groove and are a very effective means of control. They should only be used by an experienced rider with sensitive hands. Ask expert advice before fitting one.

Fitting a Bridle

Bridles come in standard sizes in a range suitable for Shetland, pony, cob and full-size horse. After selecting the one which fits your horse, make slight adjustments as necessary. Check that the bit is sitting correctly in the mouth; a jointed bit should leave one or two wrinkles at the corners of the mouth and a straight bit bar one wrinkle. Never fit a bit so tightly or so loosely as to damage a horse's teeth.

Standing Martingale

The standing martingale should be fitted to the cavesson noseband (on no account should it be fitted to a drop noseband) and should be used to prevent the horse from throwing his head beyond a controllable level. It must not be used to hold a horse's head down.

Running Martingale

The running martingale should be fitted to prevent the horse from throwing his head beyond a controllable level. Like the standing martingale, it should not be used to hold the head down.

◀ This show-jumper is wearing a snaffle bit, a grakle noseband and a breastplate with a running martingale attachment.

PROTECTIVE LEG GEAR

▼ This horse is wearing brushing-boots to protect his legs should they knock against one another while exercising.

There are many different types and brands of protective and supportive boots readily available.

Brushing-boots These can be made of leather, plastic, or foam and can be fastened with velcro or buckles. Their primary purpose is to prevent a horse from striking one leg against its opposite. They also provide a degree of protection from other knocks and bumps.

Clarendon-boots These are brushing-boots which are fleece-lined for comfort and have double fastenings for added security. They are very sturdy.

Tendon-boots Designed to protect the tendons of the front legs from a blow from a hind foot, they are commonly used to protect the legs of show-jumpers.

Overreach-boots These are usually made of rubber or plastic to protect the heel area of the front legs from a blow from a hind-leg.

Knee-boots These are vital when hacking on roads and hard ground. They protect the delicate knee area should a horse fall. Falling onto the knees can cause permanent damage.

Medicine-boots These wrap around the lower leg offering almost total protection to the whole area.

Exercise bandage Despite the state-of-the-art technology of modern boots, the exercise bandage is still used, particularly by cross-country riders. It offers maximum support to the tendons and protection against a strike from the hind foot. Once applied, the bandage should be stitched or taped into place with no tags showing.

BRUSHING-BOOT

CLARENDON-BOOT

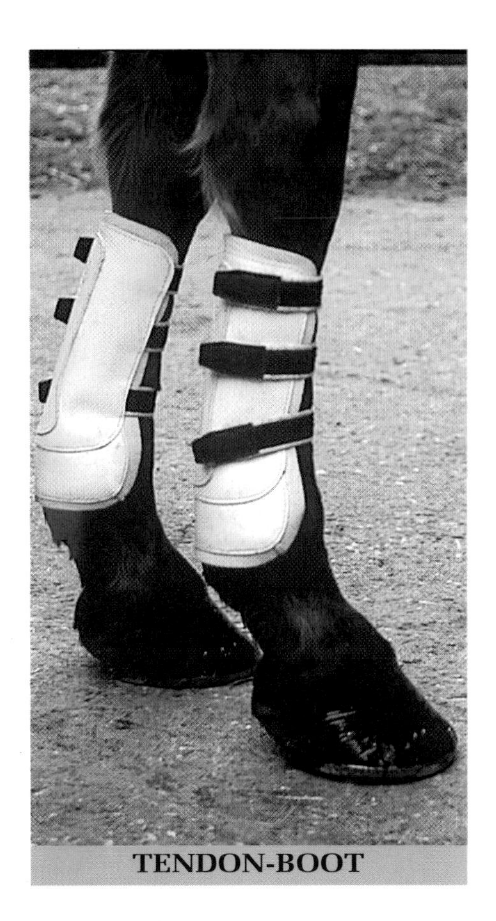
TENDON-BOOT

MEDICINE-BOOT

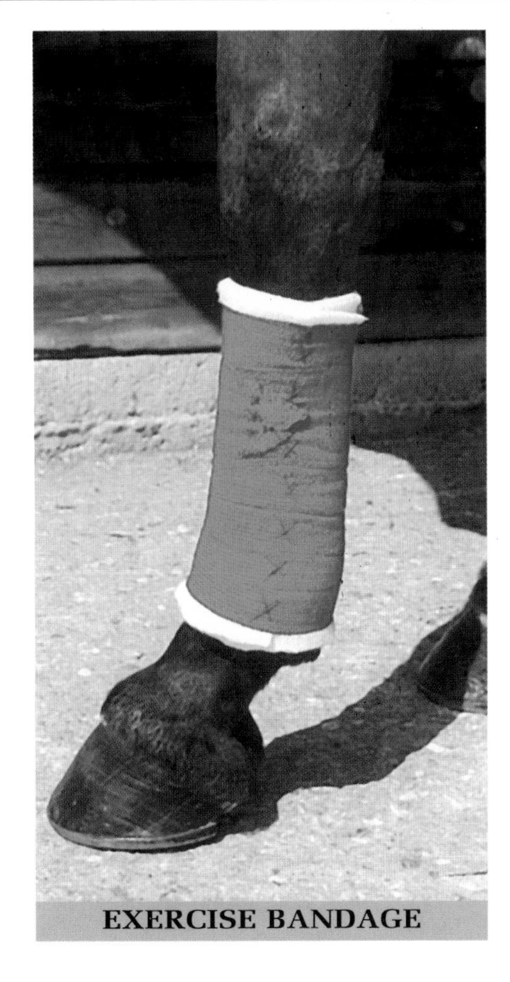
EXERCISE BANDAGE

OVERREACH-BOOT

KNEE-BOOT

TRAVELLING AND SHOWS

If you are serious in your wish to compete, you must be prepared to travel to shows using some means of transport. If you intend to buy your own trailer or box, seek expert advice before doing so.

Horses who travel regularly become quickly accustomed to being loaded and unloaded and soon learn how to keep their balance while the vehicle is in motion. Provided that the inexperienced young horse is introduced to travelling sympathetically and gradually, there is no reason why he should be alarmed in any way.

Great care must be taken when training the inexperienced horse to enter a vehicle. Protective gear should be worn by both horse and rider in order to minimize injury. Generally speaking, horses travel far better in the company of others and it is advisable for them to be accompanied by a more experienced horse which will have a calming influence on the younger one. A securely tied haynet at a safe height will also help keep a young horse occupied. Practise boxing young horses to allow them to become accustomed to the new experience. To build up confidence, practise loading and unloading over a period of a few days. Give the horse a small feed while he is inside the horsebox as a reward for his good behaviour.

▼ This horse is prepared for travelling. His is wearing bandages which cover the coronet, as well as knee-boots, a tail-guard and a poll-protector. This will enable him to be loaded and to travel in safety.

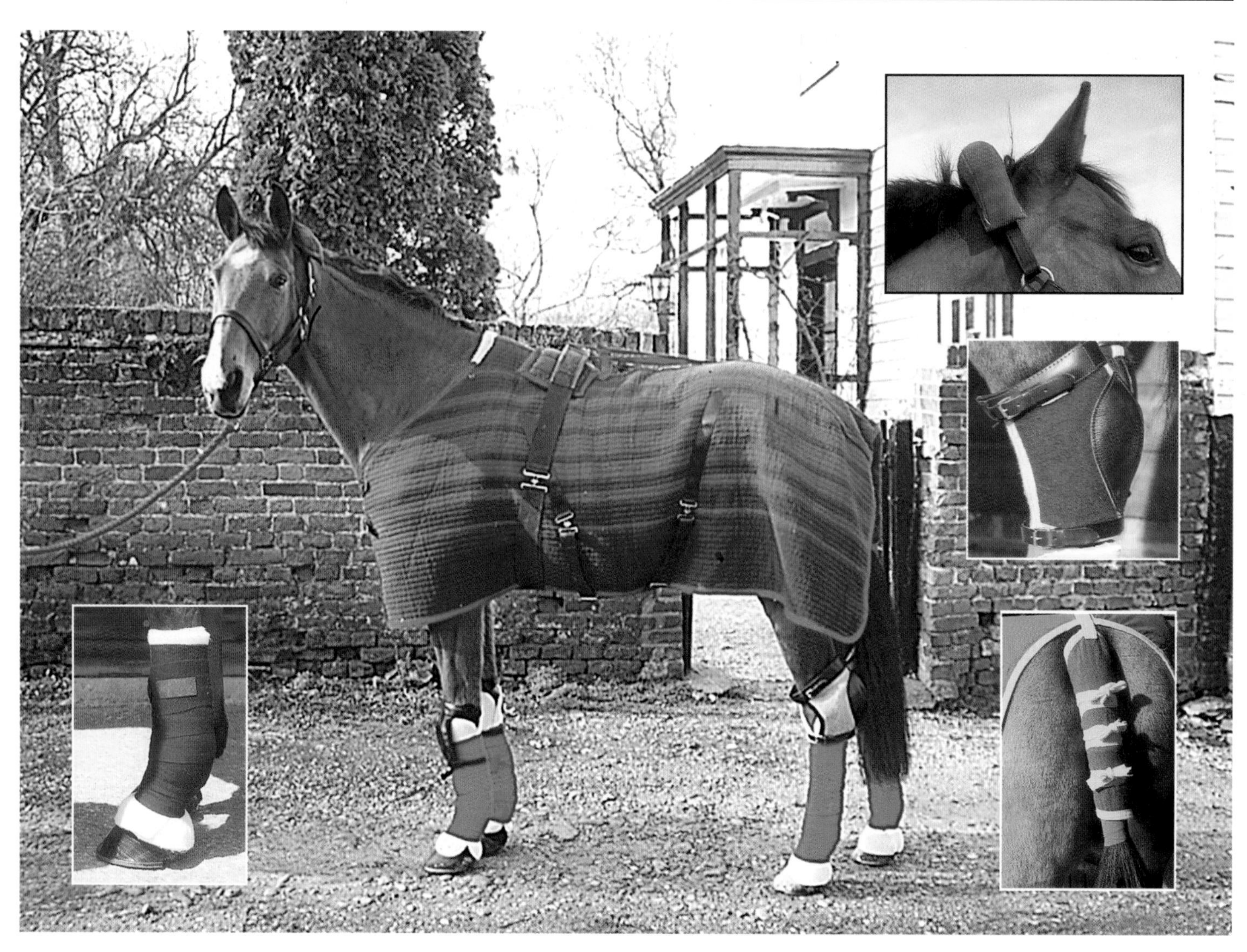

In cold weather, horses should be rugged up when travelling. However, in the confines of a horsebox or trailer the temperature can become quite elevated, particularly if horses become excited. Be careful not to put on too many rugs, as an uncomfortable horse will find it difficult to settle. A sweat sheet underneath an over-rug is the best combination, as the holes in the sheet will allow air to circulate, keeping the horse warm and dry. Make sure the rugs are securely fastened by rollers. Protective bandages over gamgee, knee-boots and hock-boots will give protection to the legs. As an extra precaution, overreach-boots can be placed on all four feet to protect the coronet band. A tail-guard will protect the tail. Last, but not least, a poll-guard attached to the headcollar will help protect the horse's head should it hit the roof of the horsebox.

PUTTING ON A TAIL BANDAGE

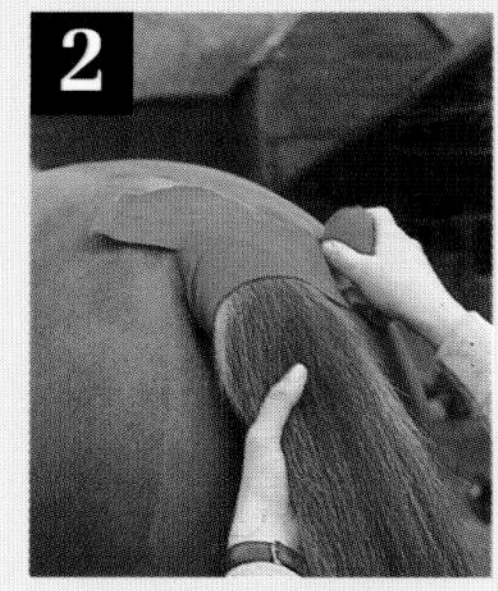

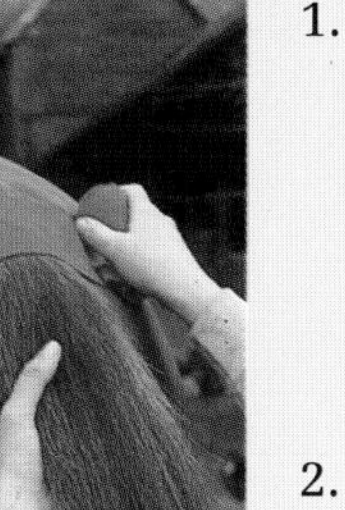

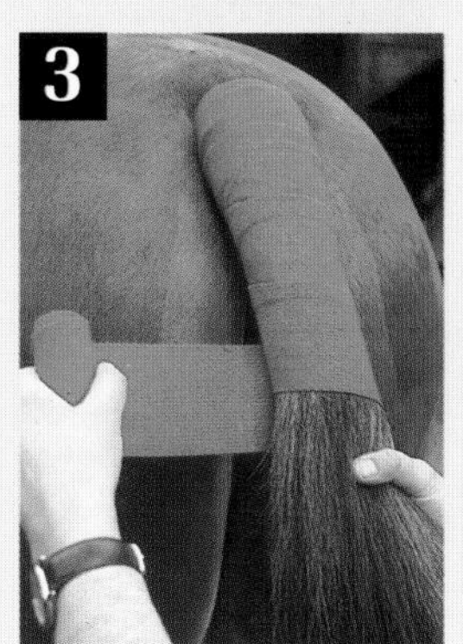

1. Roll the bandage over and under the tail, leaving a tag free.
2. Continue bandaging, turning the tag in and bandaging over it.
3. Continue until dock covered.
4. Secure with a bow. Tuck tail between legs.

LOADING UP AND TRAVELLING WITH A HORSE

- Always have a helper with you if at all possible.
- Always wear a riding hat, gloves and sturdy boots when leading, and remember never to wind a lead rope around your hand.
- Try to keep the horse straight and aim him at the centre of the ramp. Stay by his side. If he falters or hangs back, do not try to drag him up the ramp. Reassure him and give him some encouragement.
- Make sure the breeching strap or partitions are in place before tying the horse up. This can be done by your helper.
- Make sure the horse is safely tied up with a quick-release knot and that the partitions are correctly placed to prevent the horse from turning around in the box or trailer.
- Be wary of all ramps and doors. They are usually very heavy and you should avoid standing underneath them.

- Make sure that all equipment is stored away and can't fall on the horse during transit.
- Make sure that haynets are well secured and can't be pulled down.

It is usually safe to load a well-mannered, more experienced horse, wearing only a headcollar. However, a strong-willed or mischievous animal may need to be led in a bridle. Place a snaffle bridle without a noseband over the headcollar and lead the horse by taking the reins over his head, holding onto the lead rope as well. Secure the horse in the box to a tying-up ring, removing the bridle to ensure that the horse remains comfortable throughout the journey.

Some riders travel to competitions with their horses already tacked up. This is perfectly acceptable, though not advisable on a long journey; the horse's comfort should be your main priority.

It is wise to compile and consult a check-list prior to all journeys involving the transportation of horses. Take a mobile phone with you in case of emergency.

Travel check list

- Check oil, fuel and water in the horsebox.
- If towing, check towing-hitch for safety and that it is at the correct height.
- Check brakes, lights, indicators and tyres for wear and correct pressure.
- Check that the vehicle is generally roadworthy.
- Occasionally, check horsebox flooring, fixtures and fittings for soundness.

Preparing for a show

Getting youself and your horse ready for a show will require a good deal of practice and hard work to achieve the smartest of appearances. However, by following correct procedures, there is no reason why that professional look cannot be achieved.

Plaiting the mane

You will need:
A mane comb, thread in the same colour as the horse's mane, a fairly large, blunt-ended needle, a water brush and scissors.

1. Make sure the mane has been thoroughly brushed and all knots have been removed. Dampen the mane and then divide it into equal sections. These sections can be temporarily secured with elastic bands.
2. Start by the ears. Take the first section and plait/braid it right to the very end. Using the needle and plaiting thread, secure the end.
3. Turn the end of the piait under and sew in to neaten the edges.
6. Roll the plait under until it forms a small neat bobble. Make sure that it is nice and tight. When you get to the end, sew it all together trying not to let too much thread show. Finally, trim the excess thread off carefully.

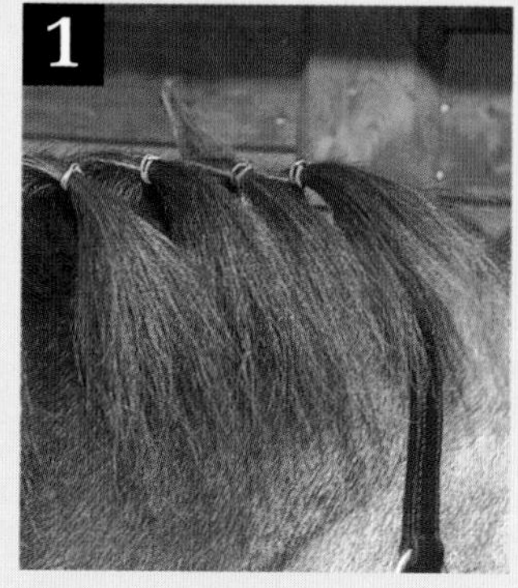

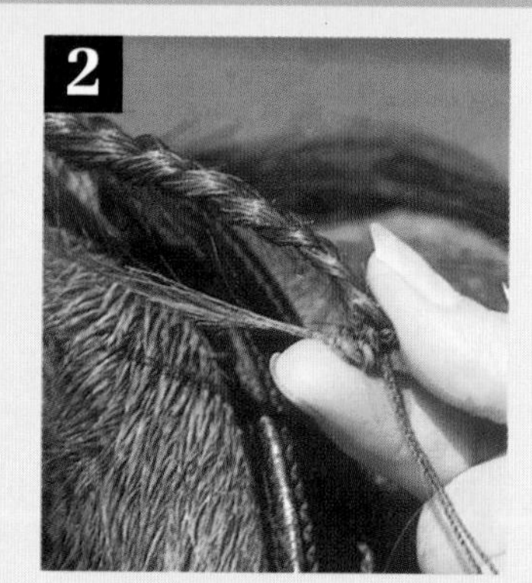

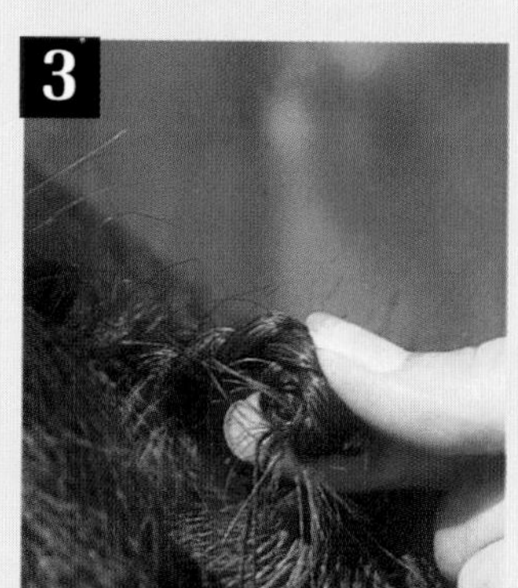

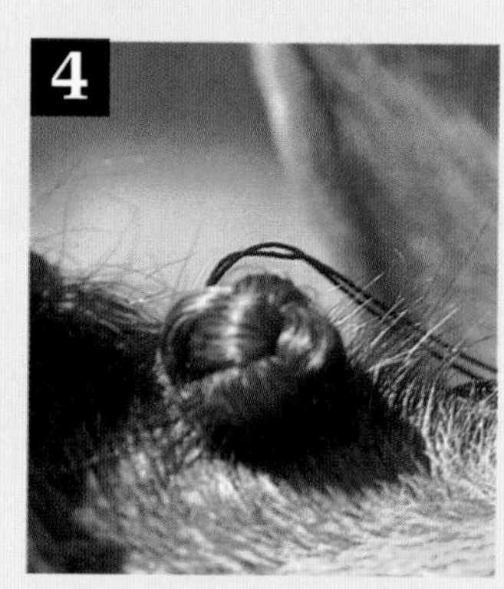

PLAITING THE TAIL

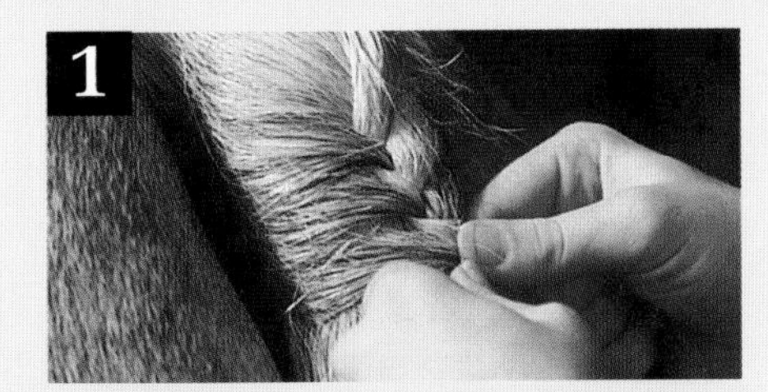

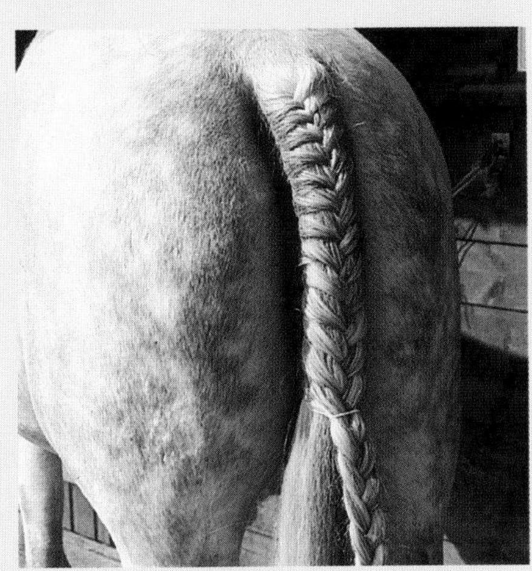

Tail-plaiting is a way of showing off the horse's hindquarters as well as giving the tail an attractive, well-groomed appearance.

1. After thoroughly brushing and combing the tail, incorporate small sections of tail hair from either side, starting at the top next to the dock to form a central plait. Continue down the tail, making sure the plait is neat and even.

2. When you reach the end of the dock, carry on plaiting the top section only until you reach the end. Turn the plait under and sew in to hide the end.

Preparing the horse

The hard work starts the day before: wash and dry all boots, numnahs and travel rugs which will be worn at the show or event.

Clean all leather tack thoroughly, making sure all metalwork is well

▲ Suddenly, every bit of hard work seems worthwhile when you get a first in the show-ring. Here, both pony and rider are immaculately presented and thoroughly deserve their rosette.

polished to a shine. Most bits and stirrup irons these days are made of stainless steel, so a soft dry cloth is usually all that is needed to buff them up. Pack as much for the next day as possible. This will make life easier when departing next day.

Make sure you are familiar with the times of your classes and check the route to the show carefully to ensure you arrive there in good time. If you are hacking to the show, allow plenty of time: you do not wish to over-exert yourself or your mount.

Give the horse a very thorough grooming. If the weather is fine you can wash the mane and tail.

On the morning of the show, the horse will need to be throughly groomed for a second time, as well as plaited. Do not plait a horse the night before as it could cause discomfort: in any case, plaits usually become untidy or come loose overnight.

Trimming The feathers on the fetlocks and around the ears and chin can be carefully trimmed; be careful not to stab either your horse or yourself. Blunt-ended scissors are essential. Do not trim the whiskers of a grass-kept animal as this could damage his sensibilities when foraging for grass.

The Rider's Dress

Many different types of outfit are worn in equestrian activities; but whatever the discipline you choose, you must be well turned-out, as well as clean and tidy.

The most essential item is the riding hat or skull-cap which must comply with the latest safety standards. A riding hat which has suffered a blow, either in a fall or by dropping, should be discarded. For cross-country, the ordinary riding hat is insufficient – a skull-cap is a must. All hats must be secured by a chin-strap at all times. Depending on what class you choose, the length of your whip is crucial. A whip that is too long can sometimes mean disqualification. Jackets and jodhpurs must be clean and tidy and leather boots must be highly polished.

For most riding club events, including dressage, showing and show-jumping, this form of dress is fine. In the case of dressage, the only thing which needs to be changed is the whip, as a long schooling whip is allowed. However, if you were to compete at top level, you would be required to wear a top hat and tailed jacket.

◀ In higher levels of show-jumping in Britain, only men wear red jackets. However, they are worn by both men and women in the United States.

◀ In cross-country events, safety is of paramount importance. A skull-cap, body-protector and sturdy gloves are vital.

INDEX